# AN ON-GOING IMAGINATION

# AN ON-GOING IMAGINATION

*A Conversation about Scripture, Faith, and the Thickness of Relationship*

## WALTER BRUEGGEMANN
### AND
## CLOVER REUTER BEAL

Edited by Timothy Beal

WESTMINSTER
JOHN KNOX PRESS
LOUISVILLE • KENTUCKY

*First edition*
Published by Westminster John Knox Press
Louisville, Kentucky

19 20 21 22 23 24 25 26 27 28—10 9 8 7 6 5 4 3 2 1

Scripture quotations from the New Revised Standard Version of the Bible are copyright © 1989 by the Division of Christian Education of the National Council of the Churches of Christ in the U.S.A. and are used by permission.

*Book design by Drew Stevens*
*Cover design by Marc Whitaker / MTWdesign.net*

**Library of Congress Cataloging-in-Publication Data**

Names: Brueggemann, Walter, author. | Beal, Clover (Clover Reuter), author.
Title: An on-going imagination : a conversation about scripture, faith, and the thickness of relationship / Walter Brueggemann and Clover Reuter Beal.
Description: Louisville, Kentucky : Westminster John Knox Press, [2019] |
Identifiers: LCCN 2019002009 (print) | LCCN 2019016104 (ebook) | ISBN 9781611649413 (ebk.) | ISBN 9780664264130 (pbk. : alk. paper)
Subjects: LCSH: Bible—Theology. | Bible—Criticism, interpretation, etc.
Classification: LCC BS543 (ebook) | LCC BS543 .B6825 2019 (print) | DDC 220.6—dc23
LC record available at https://lccn.loc.gov/2019002009

Most Westminster John Knox Press books are available at special quantity discounts when purchased in bulk by corporations, organizations, and special-interest groups. For more information, please e-mail SpecialSales@wjkbooks.com.

# CONTENTS

# FOREWORD
## *Timothy Beal*

In his teaching, preaching, and writing, Walter Brueggemann testifies to a deep and abiding relationship with the
biblical text and with the vexing, awesome, and awe-full
God who cannot be disentangled from that text, who seems
to grasp him without ever quite being grasped.

He puts on the Bible like an old coat—not a comfortable driving jacket, let alone a glorious coat of many colors,
but a well-worn, woolly, coarse and scratchy thrift store
coat that never quite fits. It pinches; it bunches and binds.
It's a little too warm in the summer and not warm enough
in the winter. And it's never really in style. Yet there's no
imagining him going out without it.

It could lead to some awkward and uncomfort-
able situations. Like in our Psalms class, when he insisted
that if the psalmist is lamenting God's absence, then God
is absent; and don't dare try to counter with the common
assurance that, well, the psalmist might feel that way, but
we know better. No, if the text gives expression to divine
absence, then that is the truth of that text. And who knows?
Perhaps the psalmist's passionate railing against this absent
and forgetful God will motivate that God to return and to
act in transforming ways on the psalmist's behalf. In one
of the conversations that formed this book, he suggested

that God in Scripture is "in recovery" from an addiction to violence.

There are a great many unforgettable, uncomfortably provocative stories of Walter Brueggemann teaching in the classroom or preaching from the pulpit. And in every case, the astonishing thing he says, whether in a whisper or at the top of his lungs, emerges from his close and careful work with the details of the biblical text.

As his student at Columbia Theological Seminary in Decatur, Georgia, I remember yearning to have a feel for the Bible like his. I also remember learning the hard way that my ways will never be his ways.

While I was completing doctoral work at nearby Emory University, Professor Brueggemann (I never dared call him Walter back then) suffered a terrible bout of shingles, and he asked me to teach his seminar on First and Second Samuel for a couple weeks while he recovered. I had copious notes from back when I had taken that seminar with him a couple years earlier. So I figured I'd just do what he did. How could I possibly do better than that? I had copied down all his spells. I would recite them, dance before the ark like he and David did, and all would go well.

It was a disaster.

I talked my way through my notes from his lectures, channeling my best Brueggemannian voice and swagger as I offered his analyses of the structures and patterns of the assigned texts. I drew them out on the chalkboard like he had, connecting words and phrases with broad strokes, circling and double-underlining key words, letting the chalk dust fly. But the students around the table were not impressed at all. They started interrupting with questions—questions I couldn't remember anyone asking when Professor Brueggemann had taught the same material in the same way. I had no good answers. Soon none of it was making sense, even to me.

Which is to say what I think Walter understands very well: that this peculiar text lives and moves and has its being in our own particular and peculiar lives, individual and corporate, as we grapple with it and try to put it on; that we need to keep one hand on the pen on the page, with all its oddity, and the other on our own passions and pains. This is what he does, and he invites us to go and do likewise. For that, I am endlessly grateful.

This book derives from a series of long conversations between Walter Brueggemann and his student and friend— and my spouse—Clover Reuter Beal. These conversations took place over the course of several years. Some were just between them, over coffee in our home. Most were held as public events at two different churches in which Clover has served as pastor: Forest Hill Church (Presbyterian) in Cleveland Heights, Ohio, and Montview Boulevard Presbyterian Church in Denver, Colorado.

The first of these conversations was a public event at Forest Hill Church in 2011. Although I hadn't thought about doing so ahead of time, I decided to record it on my phone. I am so glad I did. As I listened, it quickly became clear to me that something special was happening. The dynamic and rapport between them was different from other interviews with Walter that I had seen or heard. There was an intimacy of longtime friendship that allowed them to speak very candidly. This led, on the one hand, to fresh ways of accessing some of Walter's most challenging ideas and most influential publications. In fact, when I am trying to explain one of his key ideas or approaches in my own writing, I have found myself quoting from that first conversation rather than from his own books and articles. I began to imagine a larger book that might collect and edit this and other conversations as an ideal primer for those wanting to explore Brueggemann's work but without a clear idea about where to start. Here, for example, he speaks in particularly clear and engaging ways about his view of the reality-shaping power of language, his conviction that the central work of the church is about articulating an alternative world, his insistence that there is no biblical God outside the biblical text, and his view that Christians need to learn from Jewish modes of faith and biblical interpretation.

This tone and shape of friendship also made their conversation far more personal, even pastoral, than I had ever seen or heard in interviews with him. They were talking about his approaches to and views of Scripture and the life of faith, but those matters were tying into his own personal faith life and relationships with particular poignancy. They gave voice to a "thickness of relationship," with God and with others, that was disarmingly honest, inviting the rest of us to reflect on our own relationships. This combination of honest self-reflection and theological rigor struck me as powerfully unique to this particular conversation with this particular friend. I came to believe that we should host more of them, and that they needed to be shared. And that is the Genesis of this book: from one conversation to many, which I then edited into this collection. It is a collection of moments. Each of these moments finds Walter and Clover leaning in together on a particular theme or question about Scripture, faith, or the thickness of relationship—often all three at the same time. May these moments of conversation inspire—or provoke, as the case may be—many more conversations of your own making.

# PREFACE

*Walter Brueggemann*

It strikes me that the format of the pages that follow here—a series of conversations with Clover Beal and edited by Timothy Beal—is exactly the right genre for reflection on my work. The reason an interview is the right genre is that an interview is a conversation that involves two-way interaction. In these interviews, Clover and I have been in a two-way exchange that has, I think, moved us to new insight that has involved and impacted us both.

This way of dialogic conversation has become increasingly important to me as I have come to understand more fully that dialogic modes of interaction are crucial for the way of imagining that governs the Old Testament. The text itself is articulated as an act of imagination amid a particular lived circumstance and with the God who inhabits that particular circumstance. Thus, for example, I have proposed in my *Theology of the Old Testament* that Old Testament faith is an interaction between "core testimony" and "countertestimony" that admits of no settlement.[1] In the book of Psalms, Israel's talk with God consists of movement between praise and lament, often in the same Psalm. And behind that practice in the book of Psalms is the narrative account of Moses' two-way interaction with YHWH "face to face" (Exod. 33:11), as exemplified in Moses' remonstrations to YHWH in Exodus 32:11–14 and

Numbers 14:13–19. Conversely, after the book of Psalms, Job is commended by YHWH for speaking "what is right" in his shrill challenge to God (Job 42:7–8). The God of Israel invites and welcomes intense dialogic interaction that is honest and not deferential. We do well in our theological work, it follows, to replicate the kind of interaction that functions to permit new emergences, through the process of dialogue, that would not otherwise appear. Thus in these interviews, conversation with Clover has led me to fresh awarenesses about my work. I hope, moreover, that these exchanges will evoke the same for readers.

My learning about dialogic processes as a vehicle for new emergence is of course deeply rooted in rabbinic tradition. The rabbis understood that biblical texts can never be reduced to one meaning; through attentive imagination, the rabbis were able, always, to find fresh meanings in fresh readings. In recent time this "dialogic process" has been articulated and championed by Martin Buber, whose I-Thou insistence (popularly understood in facile ways) is a direct challenge to Cartesian positivism with its pursuit of a single and final certitude. Buber understood that life received from Thou and gladly given back to Thou is not a one-time happening but is an on-going process.[2] After Buber, moreover, Emmanuel Levinas has proposed that seeing the face of the other—a face that is constantly given new, fresh inflection—comes with fresh, nonnegotiable mandates for faithfulness.[3]

Through "many toils and snares," my work is an on-going awareness that interpretation is an open-ended enterprise that must refuse fixities and final certitudes. Indeed the Jewish tradition has deeply understood that "final interpretations" will, soon or late, lead to "final solutions." One may track current "final solutions" among us that are variously grounded in race, nationality, gender, or class; every time such finality is rooted in a "final interpretation" of a text that allows for and anticipates no newness yet to be given. As these interviews will reflect, I am still underway in discerning how deeply such dialogic open-endedness goes and how radically it must be honored. The issue is an urgent one in an ideologically propelled cultural context in which various competing parties have arrived at finality that precludes generative newness.

The matter of fresh discernment through dialogic interaction pertains in my work to three spheres that I can readily identify. First, my long years of teaching have witnessed a revolutionary transformation of the discipline of Old Testament study. When I began my study and work, historical criticism was the only methodological option. In retrospect that approach was a particular exercise of Cartesian reasoning that sought to explain away every contradiction in the text and to resolve every ambiguity in the text. Through recent decades, however, our discipline has moved beyond that critical enterprise to what Paul Ricoeur has termed a "postcritical" stance in which, after our best criticism, we may still retrieve deep meaning from the text that has not been erased by our skepticism. The compelling outcome of that move beyond historical criticism has been the legitimation of other approaches in Old Testament study, including social-scientific, rhetorical, canonical, and reader-response. The entry of marginalized people into the interpretive process has decisively eroded the hegemony of white, male, Western interpretation. As a result white male Westerners like me are in a long-term process of playing catch-up to newer methods and perspectives, always with an awareness that texts have many meanings.

2    Second, while alert interpreters have always been aware of the prophetic dimension of Old Testament ethics, our preoccupation with historical specificity and the passion for literary sources and dating texts has long distracted our attention away from the realities of economic systems, political arrangements, and religious legitimations of those systems and arrangements evidenced in the text and in the communities behind the text. Perhaps in part evoked by the economic radicality of Ronald Reagan and Margaret Thatcher in the 1980s, Old Testament study, notably led by Norman Gottwald, has moved toward systems analysis of socioeconomic systems and processes in the ancient world.[4] We have been able to see that the "urban elites" in every ancient culture depended on the production of "subsistence peasants" for the delivery of surplus wealth that made for self-indulgent living.[5] With that awareness about the dynamics of the text, we are much better able, from the text, to engage contemporary issues concerning the predatory economy in which we find ourselves. "Liberation theology" has been an important way station in the process of discernment of the urgent social justice issues of our own time, when attention to social justice in the text requires more than an occasional prophetic reference or an occasional "special Sunday" of proclamation. Rather, systems analysis makes clear that social justice in response to a predatory economy is central to the metanarrative of the Bible. Thus the explosion of "empire studies," with particular reference to the work of Richard Horsley, highlights the recurring urgency of social justice issues in the text and in our contexts of reading.[6]

3    Third, the current crisis in the Western church raises very hard questions about the style and structure of the church, its distinctive gospel claim, and its peculiar

and subversive mission in the world. With many nuances and variations, the urgent ecclesial question now before us, I propose, is the extent to which the church can witness to the deep contradiction between the summons of biblical faith and our accommodating ways in the world, or the extent to which we do better by concealing that contradiction and making the best of partnership with "the rulers of this age." This is the old question of "Christ and Culture," now posed with acute intensity, an intensity that requires dialogic engagement that cannot be foreclosed by ideological certitude on behalf of any particular party. The distinctive relationality of the covenantal tradition that runs through the Bible is a happy but demanding alternative in our current context through which we may imagine the church very differently.

My own work has been, as best I am able, to read the biblical text honestly and faithfully. "Honestly" means not to avoid or bowdlerize the hard parts. "Faithfully" means to be without pretense about the quotidian reality of our bodily existence. This honesty and faithfulness leads one to focus, more sharply in recent time, on matters of social justice with a capacity to notice the "class warfare" conducted from above, and with a readiness to see clearly how dangerous and subversive is an authentic gospel church. In all these matters, I have so much to unlearn, as do some who read these words. The process of unlearning and then learning is on-going.

That process can be effective only when we have good dialogic practice through which we may learn afresh what matters most. I am grateful to Clover Beal and Tim Beal, my well-beloved students, for their readiness to be engaged with me in that demanding on-going process. Clover, Tim, and I are greatly helped in practical ways in this

matter by David Dobson and his colleagues at Westminster
John Knox Press. It is my hope that these interviews will
be of interest and assistance to readers who are also par-
ticipants in the on-going enterprise of faithful honesty and
honest fidelity.

## NOTES

1. Walter Brueggemann, *Theology of the Old Testament: Testimony, Dispute, Advocacy* (Minneapolis: Fortress Press, 1997).
2. In a whimsical paragraph of *I and Thou* (Edinburgh:
T. & T. Clark, 1937), 97–98, Martin Buber reports on the
Thou quality of his cat:

> Sometimes I look into a cat's eyes. The domesticated animal
> has not as it were received from us (as we sometimes imagine)
> the gift of the truly "speaking" glance, but only . . . the capac-
> ity to turn its glance to us prodigious beings. But with this
> capacity there enters the glance, in its dawn and continuing in
> its rising, a quality of amazement and of inquiry that is wholly
> lacking in the original glance with all its anxiety. The beginning
> of this cat's glance, lighting up under the touch of my glance,
> indisputably questioned me: "Is it possible that you think of
> me? Do you really not just want me to have fun? Do I concern
> you? Do I exist in your sight? Do I really exist? What is it that
> comes from you? . . . The world of *It* surrounded the animal
> and myself, for the space of a glance the world of *Thou* had
> shone out from the depths, to be at once extinguished and put
> back into the world of *It*.

3. Emmanuel Levinas, *Totality and Infinity: An Essay on
Exteriority* (Pittsburgh: Duquesne University Press, 1969).
4. Norman K. Gottwald, *The Tribes of Yahweh: A Sociology
of the Religion of Liberated Israel 1250-1050 B. C. E.* (Maryknoll, NY: Orbis Press, 1979). The immediate fulcrum of
Gottwald's work was the University of California in the days of

unrest and rising social awareness about the repressions of society. Gottwald's scholarship is thick and deep, but such a context is not unimportant for his articulation of a fresh approach.

5.  In *The Sacred Economy of Ancient Israel* (Louisville, KY: Westminster John Knox Press, 2015), 202–3, Roland Boer comments on the practices of surplus wealth:

> The system of estates sought to deal with a very practical matter: how does one feed and clothe the nonproducers? Or rather, how does one enable the nonproducing ruling class to maintain the life to which its members had quickly become accustomed?

It is usual for us to slot the poor and marginated as the "nonproducers." Boer rightly inverts the matter to see that the genuine nonproducers are in the ruling class.

6.  See, for example, Richard A. Horsley, *In the Shadow of Empire: Reclaiming the Bible as a History of Faithful Resistance* (Louisville, KY: Westminster John Knox Press, 2008) and *Jesus and Empire: The Kingdom of God and the New World Disorder* (Minneapolis: Fortress Press, 2003).

# PREFACE

*Clover Reuter Beal*

I discovered Walter Brueggemann's work as a sophomore in college at Seattle Pacific University. *The Bible Makes Sense* was required reading in our Introduction to the New Testament course. Raised in a "Bible-believing" church tradition, I was already schooled in love for the Bible. I had been convinced of the importance of Scriptures in shaping one's identity as a Christian, and engaging in their complexities was (mostly) encouraged during my formative years. To be sure, utilizing them in one's devotional life was essentially mandated. We were encouraged to walk with God through the reading and study of the Scriptures. Needless to say, discovering Brueggemann's work with these texts opened up a whole new world of possibilities.

When I decided to pursue seminary and ordained ministry as a Presbyterian, my college professors encouraged me to study wherever Brueggemann was teaching. That turned out to be Columbia Theological Seminary. By that time, I was married to Tim Beal, and together we set out from Seattle, Washington, to Decatur, Georgia, to begin our studies.

Our first experience of Professor Brueggemann was as a preacher. It was in a chapel service during our intensive summer Greek school. I vividly remember his sermon. His exposition of two Hebrew verbs in Isaiah brought me to tears. I had read his books for years, yet, to be honest, I was not prepared for the profound impact his preaching and teaching would have on me. It wasn't only the brilliance of his scholarship and pedagogy but also the honesty with which he approached the text. The Scriptures clearly were texting his life, and that truth inspired me to work to communicate to mainline Presbyterians a commitment to the Scriptures that lets them shape our lives.

Tim and I were fortunate to develop a friendship with Walter over the years. His guidance and encouragement, his wisdom and care for us and our children, have moved both of us personally and professionally in ways that we cannot have imagined possible.

This book is the result of privileged opportunities I've had to engage in public conversations with Walter. It occurred to Tim and me that there were insights and reflections that Walter shared in our conversations that we had not otherwise read in his written works. We wanted to share these conversations, and the insights that emerge through them, with others. For those of you discovering the work of Walter Brueggemann for the first time, this is a terrific primer. For those who want to share Walter Brueggemann with others and need a condensed version of his thoughts on a variety of topics and themes, this will be a most helpful book.

Thank you to the members of Forest Hill Church (Presbyterian) in Cleveland Heights, Ohio, for hosting Walter Brueggemann in 2011. That visit occasioned my first opportunity for rich public conversation with him. I also thank my current church, Montview Boulevard Presbyterian Church in Denver, Colorado, for giving me two more occasions to be in discussion with Walter. I thank

Tim Beal for editing these and other conversations with Walter into a compelling book.

Most importantly, I want to thank Walter for his willingness to engage in these conversations and for allowing us to share them with others. As always, I learned a great deal from his thoughts and words, and I will continue to draw out meaning from them for years to come. I have been nourished. I trust and pray this book will nourish others as well.

# PARTY LINES AND CHURCH CAMPS
## Early Influences

**Clover Reuter Beal (CRB):** I was first introduced to your work in the early 1980s while I was an undergraduate student at Seattle Pacific University. I was in an introductory course on the New Testament, and the professor, Robert Wall, assigned your book *The Bible Makes Sense*. Published in 1977, this was one of the first books you wrote that reached a broader audience, beyond scholars. In fact, people are still reading and talking about it today. To this day I remember how powerfully it moved me. I'm sure I'm not the only one who decided to go into ministry after reading it.

I was actually a Pentecostal at the time. Sadly, women in that movement are not encouraged to enter ordained ministry, especially as solo pastors. So attending a Pentecostal seminary was not my best way forward. When I asked Professor Wall for advice, he told me, wherever Walter Brueggemann is, go there.

At that time, you were at Eden Theological Seminary, a United Church of Christ (UCC) school in St. Louis, Missouri. So I thought, well, wherever and whatever that is, I'll go there and become UCC! But then, by the time I was ready to apply, you had moved to Columbia Theological Seminary, a Presbyterian (USA) school in Decatur, Georgia. So my newlywed husband, Tim

1

(Beal), and I applied there—*only* there, in fact. You may well be the main reason we are Presbyterians!

Working with you and other wonderful professors at Columbia was a powerfully life-changing and liberating educational experience for us. Now, two decades later, we are so grateful to have moved from a professor-student relationship then to what we feel is a real friendship, even as we continue to treasure your mentoring of us.

Of course, you have many friends and colleagues, many mentees, and a great many others who have been profoundly influenced by your work.

Speaking of mentors and influences, I want you to share more of your own story. I take it your career path as an academic was not a well-trodden one where you grew up. Were you something of an anomaly in your community?

**Walter Brueggemann (WB):** Yes. Nobody from my high school went to college or anything. But my dad, who was a pastor, was adamant that my brother Edward and I would go. So I was lucky to have so much support and encouragement from my parents.

**CRB:** And how did your mother and father meet?

**WB:** Dad was a young pastor serving on the staff at summer church camp, and my mother was enrolled. He was ten years older than she.

**CRB:** Was your mom a full-time stay-at-home mom? Did she do anything else?

**WB:** Oh yes, that's what she did. She had an eighth grade education. She would have been a pastor had women been able to do that. She really was an assistant pastor to our church—not by title but by function. Do you know what a party line is on the phone?

**CRB:** Sure—a single phone line shared by multiple house-holds. That's what I grew up with. Sometimes you would pick up the phone to call someone and hear a neighbor talking to someone else. So you'd hang up and try to make your call later—or at least that's what you were supposed to do. You could also listen in!

**WB:** That's right. We had a party line, so she spent many hours listening. She'd say, "Well I have to so your dad can know what to do."

**CRB:** That's pastoral care. She was helping him keep ahead of the game! When were you yourself first drawn to the ministry? Was it while you were a student at Elmhurst College, or earlier, or later?

**WB:** That was really when I was still in high school. My father was a mentor to many younger pastors, and they were coming through our house all the time. I thought they were the neatest people in the history of the world. I think getting to know them drew me into ministry. Every summer during high school I went to church sum-mer camp, and these same young pastors were the staff for summer camp. So I got to be connected with them. That's really where my interest in ministry came from.

# A NICE PROVIDENTIAL TRAJECTORY

## *Education*

**CRB:** So you started at Elmhurst College just west of Chicago in 1951. What did you study there?

**WB:** My major was sociology, but I went to college as what we called in those days a "pre-the," or pre-theological student. Elmhurst College had a hoard of pre-the students in those days. It was the college of our denomination (United Church of Christ, or UCC) in the Midwest, so that's where we all went.

**CRB:** I would have guessed that you were an English major in college, given your very literary approach to biblical texts.

**WB:** I would have been an English major, but I was a coward. The English teachers at my school were the hardest. I didn't think I could do that. So I didn't take many English courses. I should have. My brother was a year ahead of me, and he majored in sociology, so I just kind of followed along. And then I followed him along to seminary as well.

**CRB:** Did you have any particular mentors in college?

**WB:** I had two really important college teachers. One was my sociology professor. Elmhurst was a small school, and the department of sociology was a one-man department. This guy had a passion for justice, but he was a very old line teacher. He lectured from old yellow notes, and your work on the exam was to give back things in the order that he had given them to you. That is a way I learned. Now that my son John is a professor of sociology, we talk about all that. As I recall, a great deal of what he was giving us is the same stuff that John operates with, except that Karl Marx was not on my professor's screen. So he was important; he really shaped me. I never had any kind of personal relationship with him. I think I talked to him once. But I took eight classes from him.

**CRB:** Really? You didn't talk with him outside of class, even in a small school like that?

**WB:** He didn't talk to you. You could have tried to talk to him, but why would you do that? He was probably in his sixties. This was the 1950s, and he still drove a Model-T Ford. He was a real curmudgeon.

**CRB:** And who was your other influential professor?

**WB:** My other major influence was a guy that had come from Germany forty years earlier, and managed to retain a heavy German accent. So I learned Greek from him with a heavy German accent. Years later, when I was a faculty member at Eden, I served on the Admissions Committee. This same professor would write letters of reference for every Elmhurst student that applied to Eden, and the letter always said something like, "This is a not very bright and not very diligent student who doesn't have much focus in his life. I heartily recommend him for admission." So those were my two main college teachers.

**CRB:** I can't imagine he wrote that about you when you applied! At any rate, you were accepted and went on to Eden Theological Seminary in St. Louis in 1955. Was that the pipeline—Elmhurst to Eden?

**WB:** Yes, everybody went to Eden after Elmhurst. The quip in my church was the "three Es"—Elmhurst, Eden, and Eternity. Thirty of my classmates from Elmhurst went to Eden. This was not good at all because if you got messed up relationally at college then you just carried that on into seminary.

**CRB:** Were there any women in the program?

**WB:** Not in those days, no.

**CRB:** Your brother Ed also went to Eden, right?

**WB:** Yes, yes.

**CRB:** But he didn't go on to graduate school? He was a pastor.

**WB:** No, my brother did not go to graduate school. Yes, he was a pastor and for many years a bishop-type in the UCC, a very effective leader. He was somewhat averse to books. He had always been a year ahead of me, but then he took a year-long internship after his junior year. So we were seniors together at Elmhurst. I remember we were both in a course on Paul's letter to the Romans, which was the lynchpin of the pre-the curriculum there. What some class members, including Ed, did not know was that if the teacher planned to call on you in class to read and translate from the Greek, he would forewarn you so you could prepare. When the teacher said, "Mr. Brueggemann, would you read the next verse?" I knew he was calling on me, but my brother panicked because he thought he was calling on him, and he wasn't prepared.

**CRB:** Did you have mentors at Eden?

**WB:** My main teacher, the one who propelled me to graduate school, was Lionel A. Whiston Jr. He himself published very little, but he was teaching me just as the German Old Testament theologian Gerhard von Rad was being translated into English. And it was really von

Rad that was generating my excitement. I had never heard of graduate school. I didn't know anyone went to graduate school. That had never crossed my mind. I guess it was during my middler (second) year at Eden that Whiston started prepping me. My other primary teacher there was a very dynamic systematic theologian who just taught very liberal Reformed theology. He read the entire tradition through the lens of covenant. That was not only a faithful Reformed idea, but it was very hot at the time in ecumenical circles.

**CRB:** What do you think Professor Whiston saw in you? What made him want to start prepping you for graduate school?

**WB:** Oh, I don't know. I guess that he saw that I was a disciplined student, and that I did Hebrew as best I could do Hebrew. At one point, I almost dropped Hebrew. I just couldn't figure it out. But then one day I sort of got the gestalt of it. So that was Whiston's doing.

**CRB:** So he taught you biblical Hebrew at Eden. Did you have another Old Testament professor there?

**WB:** My first Old Testament teacher at Eden was Allan Wehrli.

**CRB:** The name is familiar, because you gave my husband, Tim, Dr. Wehrli's personal copy of Hermann Gunkel's famous book, *Schöpfung und Chaos in Urzeit und Endzeit* (Creation and chaos in origin times and end times). Wehrli's name is inscribed in it from when he was a student in Gunkel's class in Germany.

**WB:** That's right. He's the only person I know who studied with both Hermann Gunkel and William F. Albright. I think with Albright late in his life, and with Gunkel when he was really defining his form-critical approach to biblical traditions. When I took Professor Wehrli's three-term-long introduction to the Old Testament, the whole first term was focused on the *Gattungen*, or "genres," that Gunkel had identified. That's all we did for a whole term. It was a perfect outline of Gunkel. Professor Wehrli also taught me Hebrew grammar, but he wasn't personally formative for me. I think he published one little book.

Allan Wehrli had a son, Eugene Wehrli, who was a New Testament scholar. He had been my advisor at Elmhurst. Then, before my senior year at Elmhurst, he joined the faculty at Eden. Later, when I was a faculty member at Eden, Eugene was my colleague. We were there together for many years. After I left, he became president of the seminary and served for seven years. He also published very little. Publishing just wasn't in the air. Nobody cared.

**CRB:** And why Union Theological Seminary for doctoral work? Why did you choose that school?

**WB:** Whiston picked Union for me. I had never heard of Union or anyplace else. He said, "You go to Union." And it was providential, because if I had gone anywhere where the focus was on Israelite and Judean history and archaeology, I probably would not have stayed. But James Muilenburg was at Union, and he was doing biblical-rhetorical criticism, which was a more literary approach, and that worked out perfectly for me. So that whole sequence from studying sociology in college, to Hebrew in seminary, to rhetorical work with Muilenburg at Union was a nice providential trajectory.

**CRB:** After your adult education class at church this morning, a woman told me she felt like she was just beginning to understand how central social and economic justice are to the gospel and to our work as the church. "I'm sixty-eight," she told me, "and I'm only just starting to get this!" She asked me if you have always "gotten it" or if it has come to you over time. Have you always "gotten it"? Or were there key moments or key influences in your journey that illuminated your convictions about God's justice and this alternative world that we confess or need to give witness to? What has been the trajectory for you?

**WB:** I was a college sophomore, I think, or maybe even a junior, and I didn't know anything. And somehow I found out about Reinhold Niebuhr. I'd never heard of him before, but I checked out his book, *Moral Man and Immoral Society* (1932). I can still remember where I was sitting when I read it. I was so shocked that I read it again.

**CRB:** Say more about that. I think a lot of readers will know a little something about Niebuhr—that he was a prominent public intellectual, and perhaps also that he has influenced political leaders like Jimmy Carter and Barack Obama as they have struggled to promote social justice within the practical realities of politics and compromise. Some might also be familiar with the idea of systemic evil, that is, the structural nature of social injustice, which means that individuals are shaped by the unjust systems they inhabit more than vice versa. But what really blew you away about that book and made you go back and read it again?

**WB:** In *Moral Man and Immoral Society* Niebuhr argued that in one-on-one relationships we are moral people, but when it comes to public conduct we are characteristically immoral people because of the reality of power in all of our relationships. That was a whole new idea to me. An ex-pacifist writing in the years before the rise of Nazi fascism, Niebuhr was a severe critic of the individual idealism that drove much of liberal thought. I suppose I was the kind of liberal to whom he addressed the book. It awakened me from my dogmatic slumbers, as Kant would have put it. So my discovery of Niebuhr was important and on-going.

Then in his great Gifford Lectures in the late 1930s, eventually published in two volumes as *The Nature and Destiny of Man* (1943), Niebuhr spent a lot of time trying to puncture American arrogance and the sense of being God's "special chosen people" and all that. He articulated what he came to call "Christian realism." The Christian part is that he believed the Gospel, and the realism part is that he took more seriously the reality of power in the world.

Niebuhr really was a household name at Eden when I was a student there. All my teachers were good friends with him. Like me, he had gone to college at Elmhurst and then to seminary at Eden. He was the chairman of Eden's Board of Trustees for twenty-five years while teaching theology at Union in New York. The lore is that Samuel Press, who was Eden's president at the time, would take the train to New York twice a year and sort of get the guidance he needed from Niebuhr about running a seminary.

Reinhold's younger brother, H. Richard Niebuhr, was also very connected to Eden. He too had gone to Elmhurst and then Eden. After graduate school at Yale Divinity School, he returned to teach at Eden. He was also president of Elmhurst College from 1924 to 1927 before going on to teach at Yale.

I don't know whether I've told you that I just got the Niebuhr Medal from Elmhurst College last year. I was the first alum to get it. You know, it's not a big deal, but it's a nice deal.

An ex-pacifist writing in the years before the rise of Nazi fascism, Niebuhr was a severe critic of the individual idealism that drove much of liberal thought. I suppose I was the kind of liberal to whom he addressed the book. It awakened me from my dogmatic slumbers, as Kant would have put it.

**CRB:** That's wonderful.

**WB:** And I'm increasingly aware of how Niebuhrian I am. On the other hand, I recently reread *The Nature and Destiny of Man*, and he doesn't know what to do with biblical text. The only text that I noticed that he cited a number of times is a text from Isaiah about the haughtiness of battle, which he translates as the haughtiness of the United States.

**CRB:** In terms of you finding your own voice as a teacher, public speaker, and writer, do you remember aha moments, light bulb moments of, "Oh, this is what I need to be doing"?

**WB:** Yes, but more so in my later years. Before that, earlier in my career as a professor, I just thought it was part of my job. I was very satisfied about it, but I didn't have a sense of destiny about it or anything. I knew I was fortunate to get to go back to my alma mater, and so I was glad about all that, but I didn't have a sense until much later that this is a perfect match for my gifts. And that has grown on me.

**CRB:** Do you remember a moment? A class where that clicked?

**WB:** I don't think I could particularly identify spots. But I do remember when Hans Walter Wolff, the great German biblical scholar, was in residence at Concordia Seminary, which is a Lutheran seminary in St. Louis. I had a lot of interactions with him even though his English was not much better than my German. He had been a young pastor in the Confessing Church, which was a movement in Germany that opposed the Nazi regime's efforts to unify all Protestants under a fascist Reich Church. I talked with him a lot about what it was like to be part of that movement as a young scholar and pastor. And I think that was very solidifying to me, to recognize that what I was doing and what we were doing in theological education really was an urgent matter. It was kind of a slow growing awareness.

**CRB:** You two published a collection of essays together, *The Vitality of Old Testament Traditions* (1975). I recall you assigning readings from that book in your Old Testament Theology course.

**WB:** We did. Well, we had some articles, and we put them together into a book. I don't mean we were best friends, but one day he very formally stopped our conversation and invited me from then on to address him in the second person using the more familiar "Du" rather than the formal "Sie," which is a big rite of passage in Germany.

**CRB:** You told a similar story in class once. As I recall, you and he were driving someplace. You addressed him as "Professor Wolff," and he asked you to pull the car over to the side of the road, looked you in the eye, and said, "Please, call me Hans Walter." Tim and our friend Tod Linafelt, now a professor of biblical studies at Georgetown University, used to joke that once they earned their doctorates you would pull the car over and say, "Please, call me Hans Walter!"

Who were your most important colleagues as a young professor at Eden?

**WB:** A very important influence was my Eden colleague M. Douglas Meeks, especially his book *God the Economist* (1989), which he was researching and writing when I was working with him. That book sought to put theology, especially the Christian doctrine of God, into direct conversation with economic theory. How should the church's teaching on theology shape its teaching on political economy and our capitalist society and vice versa? That led him to recover a metaphor for God that he finds throughout biblical tradition, namely God as an economist who is centrally concerned with the production, distribution, and consumption of goods within a just and thriving household of human society.

Beyond that book, Meeks really taught me the seriousness of doing theology. And so that made a big imprint on me. We were working together in the early 1970s during the Vietnam War protests, and there was a general atmosphere of protest among students. As a first-semester course for beginning seminary students, we put together this laboriously complex syllabus. On the first day of class, Meeks presented it and then asked, "Are there any questions?" And one student held up his hand and said, "I reject it. I wasn't consulted."

**CRB:** How funny. He felt he had been drafted against his will into your course!

**WB:** Meeks was a student of the great theologian Jürgen Moltmann, who was influential in early liberation theology. So Moltmann came to Eden very often, and I spent a lot of time on Moltmann's books, especially *The Crucified God* and *Theology of Hope*. Now I try to read them again, and I find them almost impenetrable in their Germanness! Also, in the early 1970s, I read through Karl Barth's *Church Dogmatics*. I think most of it I probably didn't understand, but I got a lot from it, and what I really got is that this is an important enterprise in which I am engaged. I got chill bumps from Barth's assertion, early in his *Dogmatics*, that we begin with *reality* and then go to *possibility*. He showed that in the modern world we have it totally backward, starting with the *possible*.

I also began reading liberation theology and Marxist criticism, largely under Meeks's influence. I knew nothing about any of that before then. Then I read James Cone, then in succession feminist criticism and theology, and gay and queer theology, and then critical theory, to which Tim and Tod introduced me. And now postcolonial criticism makes demands of all white males. I think I understand a lot of things intuitively that I don't have articulated into theory very well. So I am always behind the curve and playing catch-up. I have always read a lot, so when I became aware of something, then I would stop and spend a lot of time trying to read that literature, and so it has been. I don't think there have been any great disjunctions, but there have been some spurts of awareness along the way.

**CRB:** I think Tod and Tim feel it was you who helped introduce them to critical theory. As they recall, every time they heard about a new theoretical discourse or some emerging thinker that they needed to read about, they would go to the library to check it out and find on the library card that you had already checked it out and read it!

**WB:** I was so disappointed when the library went to a system where you could no longer recover the history of a book's readers. I always thought it was so interesting and instructive to be able to trace the local "reading history" of a book.

# LUCK AND HAPPENSTANCE
## *Gaining Notoriety*


**CRB:** Most would probably say that your first break-through book was *The Prophetic Imagination* (1978). What was the genesis of that?

**WB:** I first gave it as a lecture to the UCC clergy in St. Louis. When I gave that lecture, the president of our seminary, who was not a scholar, said, "Boy, it would have taken me a couple weeks to write that." He intended it as a compliment! Then I presented the full manuscript of what would become the book at a clergy conference at North Park Seminary in Chicago. I had published a few things before that, including *The Land* (1977). Other than that, I hadn't published anything that was generative of my own work. It was only then that I began to find my "voice."

**CRB:** When did you really begin to focus on writing and publishing? Was it something you aspired to all along?

**WB:** Not at all. I think I taught seven years at Eden before it ever occurred to me to publish anything. Then I became dean, and the good fortune of that was that I got a secretary. Then when I left the deanship, they let me keep the secretary. Then when I got called to Columbia, I said I could not come unless I had a secretary. So I was very, very fortunate. I wouldn't have gotten nearly as much done without that support.

**CRB:** When we were in seminary, I remember you hired our friend and fellow student Tod Linafelt, who's now a professor at Georgetown, to clean your house every week or two. He said he would find pages of early typewritten drafts of things you were working on. We thought that was like a treasure trove and joked that we should be taking them out of the trash and publishing them under our names. It was mostly Tod's idea, of course.

Would you say that your thinking emerges as you write, or do you write what you have already been thinking? Does writing lead your thinking or record your thinking?

**WB:** I think it's a lot of the former. The writing, the actual writing process, very often is generative for me. I don't know where it is going until I start writing. It helps for me to do it all in longhand, letting me feel the words "being given." From the outset I have written everything in longhand. Sometimes I begin with an outline, but then the outline doesn't always determine how the writing goes.

---

The writing, the actual writing process, very often is generative for me. I don't know where it is going until I start writing.

---

**CRB:** So when you were writing *The Prophetic Imagination*, did you do the exegetical work on the biblical texts first and then write the book? Or were you doing the exegetical work while you were writing the book?

**WB:** I was doing it as I went along. I think that manuscript revolves around six theses, so I first had clarity about the theses, and then I asked what texts would help that along.

**CRB:** Sounds like the interpretive papers you used to assign in seminary! Pick four to six texts and move through them toward a theological interpretation.

**WB:** Exactly!

**CRB:** What about in terms of getting noticed by other scholars for your work? Do you have a sense of when your reputation as a biblical theologian really started to take off? Tim and I first studied with you at Columbia Theological Seminary in the fall of 1988. You'd only been there for a couple of years, and you'd been on sabbatical for one of them. As I mentioned earlier, I was basically told by my college mentors to go to seminary wherever you were teaching. So you definitely had some notoriety by then. I think your *Prophetic Imagination* and *Message of the Psalms* (1984) were getting a lot of praise, and we already mentioned *The Bible Makes Sense*. Our sense in the late eighties was that you were getting more and more invitations to lecture and preach around the country. As you look back, how do you think your reputation grew?

**WB:** Oh, it's very strange how that happened. A big factor in my maturation as a scholar was Doug Meeks, whom we talked about earlier. He was my colleague at Eden for about fifteen years. He really taught me the seriousness of doing theology. And that made a big imprint on me.

I think such notoriety is a lot of luck and happenstance. You get a certain review of something you've published. Then somebody notices that review, and then you get invited to do some lectures or preach. And, you know, you get more attention. I know my work is not better or worse than dozens of other people, but you get a bunch of breaks along the way and all of a sudden, you're noticed. One day you're like Willy Loman in *Death of a Salesman*. Then the next day you're "known"!

**CRB:** In 1989, you gave the esteemed Lyman Beecher Lectures on Preaching at Yale Divinity School. Those lectures were published as the book *Finally Comes the Poet: Daring Speech for Proclamation* (1989). That seemed to raise your profile quite dramatically.

**WB:** I don't know why I got invited to do the Beecher Lectures, but the fact that I got invited to do them was certainly a big deal for my reputation. The Beechers were very, very intimidating for me. The first of the four lectures started with an academic procession, like a pageant. And as we were standing in line to process, some faculty member—I don't know who it was—said, "I suppose you have lusted after this for a long time."

**CRB:** "Lusted"? That's the word he used?

**WB:** That's the word he used. I have thought of many clever responses since.

# A GOOD-ENOUGH GOD
*Personal-Theological Work*

**CRB:** The titles of those four Beecher Lectures say a lot, I think, about what you were working on in your teaching and writing in the late '80s and early '90s when I was your student. Here are their titles:

"Numbness and Ache: The Strangeness of Healing"
"Alienation and Rage: The Odd Invitation to Communion"
"Restlessness and Greed: Obedience Forms the Missional Imagination"
"Power and Dream: A Permit to Freedom"

You use very poetic language, rich with words that elicit feelings of angst, tension, struggle, and pain, but also imagination and hope. I recall your lectures in courses on the Psalms and Jeremiah being rich with similar language. At the same time, you were doing your own psychotherapeutic work, and sometimes in class you reflected on how psychotherapy can access similar internal tensions and struggles. Years later, your *Theology of the Old Testament* seemed, in many ways, to bear the fruits of that kind of critical reflection, especially in its attention to the character of God as "multilayered and conflicted."

Did your own personal work in psychotherapy change or otherwise influence your theology?

**WB:** I think that through that process, which was a long process for me, I became more aware of how it's relational right down to the bottom. That has caused me, as much as I am able, to give up essentialist categories and embrace the fact that it's all relational. I also came to terms with my flaws and wounds, realizing that they're not anything to be outgrown; they are just to be lived with.

When I began psychotherapy, I was discovering the work of Donald Winnicott, who was an English pediatric psychoanalyst. He moved beyond Freud's accent on the internal processes of id, ego, and superego and focused on the dyadic transaction between the baby and the mother, or whoever played the role of the mother. (It could also be the father, but he talked about the mother.) He said that, for a child to become healthy, the mother must at first totally give herself over to the child. He called this the "holding environment." But then the mother must know strategically the time to begin to withdraw that from the child, so that the child begins to discover that the mother has a life of her own and does not exist solely for the child.

Winnicott said there are no perfect mothers, but, as he famously put it, there are "good enough" mothers, good enough to do this work. A "good-enough" mother is at the same time adequate and flawed. But if a mother is dysfunctional, or doesn't want the child, and therefore cannot give over to the child, then the child discovers that fact within two weeks. So you, the child, begin to fake it with the mother to get what you want from her that she does not freely give. And so you develop a false self if you have a false mother.

This way of understanding that dyadic relationship between mother and child became helpful for me in two ways. First of all, it became helpful with my therapist, who was "good enough" for me. I think the extraordinary thing was that he had no judgmental dimension. Second, I transferred that developmental understanding to theology, to my experience of the Gospel God. The Gospel God is "good enough" even though the script says this God is capable of great anger. That is, the God of Israel is adequate but surely flawed and not "perfect." So that gave me categories to process, and then it helped me as I reflected on my growing up in childhood about the places of good enough and not good enough, and all that. So that was almost as helpful to me as the actual transaction in therapy, which I was doing at the same time.

The theological part of that is very difficult for people in our culture who are inured to Greek notions of perfection.

---

I think that through that process [psychotherapy], which was a long process for me, I became more aware of how it's relational right down to the bottom. That has caused me, as much as I am able, to give up essentialist categories and embrace the fact that it's all relational. I also came to terms with my flaws and wounds, realizing that they're not anything to be outgrown; they are just to be lived with.

---

**CRB:** Was therapy a challenge for you?

**WB:** What I think is right is that my public self is full of
confidence, but my personal self is not, was not. And I
think in therapy I grew in my personal self to have more
confidence. My own read is that my first marriage failed
(it was very complex, but basically) because I didn't
have enough of a liberated self to hold up my end of the
deal. And obviously all of that has fed into my exegetical
work with the biblical text, and my attempt to exposit
the Gospel God and all that. I think the Gospel God
very often is just barely good enough.

# MULTILAYERED AND CONFLICTED
*The Bible Makes Different Sense*


**CRB:** Let's talk about the Bible. You begin your well-known book *The Bible Makes Sense* with these words: "It is strange that the Bible is our most treasured book, and yet it seems so difficult that we don't find it very helpful. Perhaps we have expected the wrong things of it; we have asked of it what it cannot do. The Bible cannot be a good luck piece to bring God's blessings. Nor can it be an answer book to solve our problems or to give us right belief."

My sense as a clergy person is that today, as then, many of us are still struggling with this same problem: the Bible feels difficult, and unhelpful, even irrelevant—precisely because we still want it to be that good luck charm or answer book, and it just refuses to work that way. It has been three decades since you wrote that in *The Bible Makes Sense*. I have to wonder, what, if anything, has changed? How do you think the Bible is faring in the church these days? How are we doing?

**WB:** I wrote that book as a series of ten little articles on the Bible for a Catholic publisher, St. Mary's Press, in the wake of the Second Vatican Council, when Roman Catholics were first starting to read the Bible on their own. So it was written in that context.

**CRB:** There's an updated edition of it, right?

**WB:** Yes, but it's not much changed. They asked me to write a new foreword for it, so I did. They wrote back and said, "Well, you said the same thing that you did in the first foreword." And then when they republished it, they left them both out.

I think there is a huge hunger in our society and in the church for what the Bible offers. But there are also huge barriers that block our access to it. One of the barriers is the large apparatus of biblical historical criticism that has bamboozled people.

**CRB:** We'll come back to that.

**WB:** The other barrier for very many people, especially progressives, is the force of modern Enlightenment rationality. They want to get to the Bible, but then they are put off by the fact that the Bible does not fit with the modern rational categories through which they want to receive it. So it takes a lot to get past these barriers. Specifically, the Bible features God as a real character and a lively agent—very difficult categories for modern rationality.

**CRB:** So we could say that the Bible makes sense, but not the sense we expect. The Bible makes *different* sense.

**WB:** That's right. It is very hard work in our society and in the church to get to the news that the Bible wants to bring about this God who does not fit any of our categories. And that is what you are up to, and that is what I am up to.

---

It is very hard work in our society and in the church to get to the news that the Bible wants to bring about this God who does not fit any of our categories. And that is what you are up to, and that is what I am up to.

---

**CRB:** The Bible is not univocal. It is *polyvocal*, many-voiced, and its different voices are often in conflict with one another. And when we pay attention to its different voices, and don't try to make them all get along and agree, we begin to see that there are real tensions, even contradictions, among them. Sometimes you can see such tensions even within a single small piece of text.

**WB:** Yes. For example, in Jeremiah 4, the prophet is pounding away in poetry that essentially says that Jerusalem is going to be destroyed. He says it many ways, but then at the end of the unit, God says, "But I will not make a full end to them" (4:27). So who put that in there? It is as though God had a second thought. That's what we do with our kids. After ranting against them, we say, "But you know I love you." Perhaps that last line was added later. I can imagine a planning committee might have said, "This text is too harsh. We cannot leave that. We need to tone it down a little. So put, 'I will not make a full end to it.'" But then, when we interpret the text, we have to ask, should we give our attention to that last line, or should we pay attention to the main body? And you can see little contradictions like that turning up everywhere in the biblical text.

**CRB:** You say those tensions are carried into the New Testament as well. How so? Are there tensions and contradictions there as well? Is it too multilayered and conflicted? It seems like many Christians are able to see and accept tensions and conflicts in the Old Testament but not in the New Testament. It's as though it's okay to talk about God that way, but not Jesus!

**WB:** I think that a big tension in the New Testament is the tension between, on the one hand, the trajectory of

purity, which believes you can determine who is quali-
fied to belong, and, on the other hand, the trajectory of
generous debt cancellation, in which the text works at
saying that everybody is entitled to belonging. In the
Epistles, I suppose it's the on-going tension between
faith and works. Different letters give that tension different articulations. So how you negotiate it depends on
where you've been theologically. If you grew up in a theology of cheap grace, then you want to be a liberal that
tells people to get out and do something. If you grew
up in a church of works righteousness, then you want
to talk about grace. "Quit nagging me so much; just tell
me about God's love." So there are all these negotiations
that take place every time we interpret. And I think the
preacher has got to try to be aware of the preacher's own
propensity about this, on the one hand, while also paying attention to who is out there in the congregation and
what they're struggling with. Preachers have to try to
negotiate that. It's a complex operation.

# HEBREW BIBLE OR OLD TESTAMENT?

*What to Call It*

**CRB:** Here's a practical question that many of us wrestle with: what do we call the collection of Hebrew Scriptures in our Christian Bibles? "Old Testament"? "Hebrew Bible"? "First Testament"? "Jewish Scriptures"? "TaNaK" (an acronym for its three main parts, Torah, Nevi'im, and Ketuvim)? Something else? Many say that the term "Old Testament," which points it toward the "New Testament," implies a kind of supersession or replacement of it as "old law" by the "new law" of the gospel. With other Christians you usually call it "Old Testament." Can we talk about that?

**WB:** I learned that from biblical scholar Brevard Childs, who insisted that Christians always read the two testaments together. So the use of "Old Testament" is an acknowledgment that it is connected to the "New Testament," and that they are to be read together. So it is a confessional statement as a Christian to say "Old Testament," which obviously does not mean obsolete or superseded. Rather it refers to the foundational materials out of which the Jesus movement has come. And what is clear is that Jesus is a child of those Scriptures and that Jesus and the New Testament cannot possibly be understood except in the context of the Old Testament.

In the mid-second century, in response to Marcion, who rejected the Old Testament and its God as the wrathful and legalistic antithesis of the Christian God, the church decided that we could not get along without the Old Testament. But I think most Christians are practicing Marcionites, because we have such mistaken caricatures of the Old Testament as law and wrath and all that kind of stuff. And the only people who could possibly think that are people who have not read the text. So I suspect the phrase "Hebrew Bible" wants to give those Scriptures back to Jewish tradition and just focus on the New Testament. But what we have to insist upon is that those texts are the fount from which comes both Judaism and Christianity. So we share those texts. Someone said that Christians reading the Old Testament is like reading other people's mail. But it's not other people's mail; it's our mail, too.

Another practical problem with calling it "Hebrew Bible" or "Hebrew Scriptures" is that it's not all Hebrew—there is also some Aramaic in it. Not to mention that the Gospel writers seem to have been reading it in Greek. So it's a misnomer in any case. But I think the grounds for Christians calling it the Old Testament are above all theological: that Jesus, in Christian confession, is the embodiment and the fulfillment of the hopes of the earlier Scriptures, and I think it is essential that we make that confession.

**CRB:** When you're talking to a primarily Jewish audience, do you still use "Old Testament"?

**WB:** No, in deference I probably would not do that because it's not an appropriate context in which to make the confessional statement. On the other hand, I don't think that anyone who is Jewish is deceived by Christians using other phrasing. They know what we're up to. We Christians are reading it in terms of the Jesus movement, no matter what we call it. And I think that a lot of churches and pastors who use "Hebrew Bible" have no sense of that canonical connection. So it's a misrepresentation that's based on a misunderstanding, I think. It is an unsettled question in any case, but I think we have to think theologically about it because it isn't the phrase "Old Testament" that is objectionable to Christians; it's the whole christological claim that is objectionable, and you can't really change that by using some other phrasing.

# ALTERNATIVE LITERALISM
## *Losing Our Bible Baggage*

**CRB:** Here's another hot-button Bible topic: literalism. A lot of progressive-leaning Christians are uncomfortable with the idea of taking the Bible "literally." We are not literalists, we say, but we still want to take the text seriously, to engage with it. I think both laity and clergy are left wondering, how then do we approach it? Why are we so averse to being literal with the text? Are you a biblical literalist?

**WB:** I believe we have confusion about the word "literal." I am a literalist, by which I mean, I want to pay attention to the letter of the text. But what most mean by biblical literalism is an ideological commitment to it as historically reliable and scientifically respectable—that every word is literally true, historically and scientifically accurate, and without error. That's not really what the word literalist means, but that's what it has come to mean. So I don't want to engage in any of that. I want to be a literalist to say, "Let's see what's written there." And then, as with any good literature or any love letter or any significant writing, we maximize what is written there. So you get a love letter, and you extrapolate what else she might have meant when she wrote that. She may or may not have thought all that, but I'm going to grant it to her.

So that, if you get the letters down, the words, the sentences, then you begin to maximize it, as we do with all poetry, to see what it all means. But you've got to start with what's there.

Most of the arguments about biblical literalism are not about that at all. John Dominic Crossan and Marcus Borg are trying to emancipate us from that other kind of literalism, and I am in agreement with them on the need to do that. Borg's work in particular is a huge help to people who grew up in authoritarian fundamentalism, as did he. But that does not excuse us from the responsibility of paying attention to what is in fact happening in these words or in these sentences, so I think we need to be attentive about how we think about being a "literalist."

**CRB:** Borg's famous subtitle to his *Reading the Bible Again for the First Time* was *Taking the Bible Seriously but Not Literally*. That resonates with many of us liberal types, especially those of us carrying around what I like to call "Bible baggage" from our more "literalist" pasts. One of Borg's characteristic moves is to shift from reading biblical texts literally, as if the stories they tell literally happened, to reading them metaphorically, as offering new ways of seeing the world.

**WB:** That's right. Once Borg's wife, Marianne Wells Borg, who was at the time a canon at Trinity Cathedral in Portland, Oregon, invited me there to preach. The lectionary text was about the resurrection, so that's what I preached. Marcus generously took me out to lunch afterward, and he said, "That was a fine sermon, but none of those people understood you meant it at all as a metaphor."

**CRB:** Did he really say that?

**WB:** Yes. Yes. I think Marcus always thought that I agreed with him about everything.

**CRB:** What did you say?

**WB:** Well, he was buying lunch, so I didn't say anything.

**CRB:** During a Q&A session following one of your recent lectures, I remember someone standing up and asking, "Are we hearing you correctly, that you actually believe that this God acts, intervenes in history?" And you said, "Yes." And I heard an audible collective gasp in the room. When I talked with the woman afterward, she said, "I'm still dealing with that."

**WB:** Well, it is a hard, hard question. What I should have said was that, if you accept this narrative, then the answer is yes. You can't have this God without this narrative. But if God doesn't act or cannot potentially act, then the whole business of prayer is out the window. Because there's not someone to address who can respond. I understand why it's so difficult. So I think our situation in the church today is that we are caught between the normative narrative of the Enlightenment and the normative narrative of the Gospel, and we do not want to choose between them. And critical scholarship on the Bible, until the last generation, just mumbled about this. As part of a confessing church that wants to dispatch people in mission for justice, we cannot let go of our biblical rhetoric and the gospel, or simply reduce

---

The problem is that both liberals and conservatives are very deeply committed—as am I—to the Enlightenment narrative without even knowing it. So what conservatives do is compartmentalize, and what liberals do is mumble.

it to something more palatable to the normative narrative of the Enlightenment. I think we're stuck adjudicating those two narratives. And the problem is that both liberals and conservatives are very deeply committed—as am I—to the Enlightenment narrative without even knowing it. So what conservatives do is compartmentalize, and what liberals do is mumble.

# NOT WHAT IT MEANS
# BUT HOW IT WORKS

*Bible as Rhetoric*


**CRB:** You're saying something different here from what Borg meant by literalism. In educating our congregation and clergy, we are invited to address those obstacles— that "Bible baggage"—that keeps us from engaging the text seriously *and* literally, and to break down those obstacles and to get engaged in the literal words of the text.

**WB:** Yes, because if you take that other notion of literalism, which undergirds so much of that "Bible baggage," what you always do is read toward a conclusion: "What does this text mean, morally or dogmatically or doctrinally?" But if you take literalism this way, then you don't ask, "What does it mean?" You ask, "What is this text doing? What is this text performing?" Which is very different from trying to reach a conclusion. Your colleague John Lentz and I were just talking about how most of the commentaries are still fighting those literalist battles from the nineteenth century, and so they are practically no help at all for the preacher or for anybody of faith.

And I think the clue to being able to engage is to stop asking "What does the text mean?" and start asking, "How does it work? What is the text doing? How do the parts interact with one another to create a field of imagination?" That's what I try to do with my students,

34

and it's also what I try to do in adult education classes in churches. Let's look at a small piece of text together to see how words and images recur, revealing patterns and a kind of shape and structure that works to create a certain rhetorical effect. What is it doing, over against other possibilities? What is its vested social interest, and how does it work to promote that interest? And I think that kind of work just takes patient attentiveness to the text. You cannot do the Bible with Cliffs Notes. You have to really get into it, to work on small portions of it, to live with the text, and to see where it takes you in your imagination.

What I notice about so much Old Testament scholarship is that it rarely goes inside the text to see how the parts of the text are interacting. I think particularly in Hebrew, it's not linear. You don't just go from beginning to end and then you're done. The rhetoric is nonlinear and disjunctive, so it is creating a dramatic map of social reality. Which is why you cannot simply summarize or systematize it; you have to let the text do its thing. So you look for repeated words, images, and metaphors, and you attend to how these repetitions and patterns give shape and intentionality to the text.

**CRB:** You make it sound easy.

**WB:** No, it's not easy. But it is interesting. For example, not so long ago I was working on Psalm 35, which is a lament psalm. As I often do, I began by looking for repetitions. At three points in that fairly long psalm in my English translation (it turned out to be somewhat different in the Hebrew), the psalmist says, "Then" followed by an act of praise. "Then my soul will rejoice [v. 9] . . . Then I will thank you [v. 18] . . . Then my tongue will tell of your righteousness [v. 28]." That's three times. Which means, in this psalm, that I am *not* going to praise you until you answer my prayers and do something for me; I am going to withhold my praise from you until I see some action on my behalf. That's how the psalm works. But if you just try to work with the genre as a prayer for deliverance rather than paying attention to how the words work, then you miss all that. That is why these texts are inexhaustible: because every time you look at them, you see something else.

# RESISTING FINAL SOLUTIONS
## *Bible Study*

**CRB:** Say a little bit more about that. For example, this coming year our adult education program is launching a "Back to the Bible" program in which we are trying to reclaim the biblical text. So how shall we study it? What do you recommend? What advice do you give us as we begin that new program?

**WB:** Well, you know, I don't know how you project doing that. But I would suggest that the key to each class session is to get a small piece of biblical text in front of you, get a leader who has done some study to open the text, and then ask, "What do you see going on here?" In my experience, it often happens that people see things in the text that I had not seen in the same way before. When you get a circle of people who are serious about the text, people begin to see stuff. And the text is accessible for that, if only we can slow down enough to let it happen. It requires patience, because we are used to skimming things, and summarizing things, and reducing everything to 280 characters. (I don't know how anyone does that, but I've heard that's something people try to do.) And you cannot read any text that is important in that way. You have to invest some attentive energy into it. And if you have some other people with you who are

also investing energy into it, then I do think it gets to be
fun and it gets to be generative.

Jewish rabbinic tradition is built on the belief that a
text always has more interpretations. I think the rabbis
knew that if you arrive at a final reading, it will produce
a "Final Solution." Those like the Nazis, who arrived
at the Final Solution, want to eliminate everyone who
doesn't sign on, which means Jews. The search for a
Final Solution is a huge Christian temptation.

# DOXOLOGICAL IMAGINATION
*Creation, Science, and Truth*

**CRB:** As you know, one of the fastest growing religious groups in the United States today is the "nones," that is, those who check the "none" box on a form asking for their religious affiliation. Tim has a lot of those students in his college classes at his secular, STEM-oriented university. But he finds that they really get into it when they get to play with biblical texts, focusing on the rhetoric and how the texts work and not worrying about whether this looks anything like what God or biblical religion are supposed to look like. They find it exciting. They're taken in by approaching these texts with the kind of rhetorical-critical alternative literalism that he learned from you.

Speaking of literalism—the other kind, anyway—I imagine that another question a lot of people ask Old Testament professors like yourself is, "Is the creation story in Genesis really true?" How do you deal with questions like that?

**WB:** I think that the creation story in the first chapter of Genesis is a poetic doxology that imagines what the world is like if it is indeed God's creation. And I think that act of doxological imagination can be set alongside competing statements about the nature of the world. What is implied in that, of course, is that it is not a scientific description. Because the Bible is not really about scientific description or explanation in any way. But it is everywhere interested in doxological imagination. What is the world like if it is true that, as we say in the United Church of Christ, God calls the worlds into being? So this is an invitation for someone to think about what it would be like to practice doxological imagination.

I suppose if you have someone who is struggling with whether this story is compatible with scientific research on the origins of the universe, geological time, and evolution, then perhaps that answer could be disconcerting and unhelpful. But the truth of the matter is that the church has staked everything on doxological imagination.

---

I suppose if you have someone who is struggling with whether this story is compatible with scientific research on the origins of the universe, geological time, and evolution, then perhaps that answer could be disconcerting and unhelpful. But the truth of the matter is that the church has staked everything on doxological imagination.

---

**CRB:** I think the best of theology understands this too. It understands that theology is poetic, the work of doxological imagination rather than rational accounting or logical explanation.

**WB:** In the Episcopal church, we say the Nicene Creed every Sunday. I wish we had some variations, but that's what we do. And we say "God from God, light from light, true God from true God, begotten, not made," and so on. What the hell does that mean? It means there is something going on here that is bigger than any of our words, so we recite poetry. But what happens is some right-wing Presbyterians forget that it's poetry and want to turn it into a logical syllogism. And then you can have a trial for heresy.

So I think we have to teach our kids that the whole operation is an act of doxological imagination. And they need to understand that what we know about science is set in the middle of that. Science is of course very important, but our best scientific learning is in the environment of that kind of poetry.

# CRITICAL IS NOT ENOUGH

## *Getting to Postcritical*

**CRB:** The other day you and I were meeting with a small group of evangelical pastors in Denver. Several had at least some seminary education, but mostly in a conservative context that was largely dismissive of critical biblical scholarship. In that conversation, you said that we need to take readers, and ourselves too, from precritical to critical to postcritical stages in reading the text. Can you say more about that? Is that part of your own interest in moving beyond the now traditional historical-critical methods? What allowed you to make this shift?

**WB:** Well, I think I slowly grew aware of the need to move beyond those methods, but I discovered the succinct formulation of it in the philosopher Paul Ricoeur's schema of precritical, critical, and postcritical. Many Bible believers are precritical: that is, they essentially see the Bible as the infallible word of God. They do not subject biblical tradition, or their ideas about it, to critical methods that locate different parts of the text within their social and historical contexts, and then to reconstruct its literary development. They do not, in other words, put the Bible within the context of history; instead, they put history within the context of the Bible. The postcritical, on the other hand, understands the importance of the critical and accepts the impossibility of remaining in that precritical state of mind after subjecting the Bible to its methods. But it does not stop there. It seeks to go "beyond the desert of criticism," as Ricoeur puts it, into a "second naiveté," an "innocence" that is deeply informed by critical thinking.

When I discovered Ricoeur's formulation, I suddenly figured out that what I'm really doing, that what I'm really wanting to do, is postcritical. But you know, when I went to graduate school none of this was on the horizon. I think James Muilenburg was inching toward it with his rhetorical criticism. The historical-critical canon was totally normative, and that was all I knew. You couldn't get published and you couldn't get tenured if you didn't live in that world. If you go back and look at articles from those days in the *Journal of Biblical Literature*, which is the flagship journal of our guild, the Society of Biblical Literature, they are dreary. So it took me a long time to get some distance from it. I don't think I'm there, but I'm working on getting reeducated about all of that.

Lots of progressives have been very eager to move from the precritical to the critical, so you read Dominic Crossan and Bart Ehrman, Marcus Borg, people who do that job very well. But Bart Ehrman, for example, stops there. He does not want to make any postcritical move to say, "After I understand the critical analysis of the text, I may move beyond that to ask, Is this still the good news of the gospel that funds my life?" So I think it's very useful for all of us to pay attention to where we are on that pilgrimage from the precritical, which assumes it all fits together, and Moses wrote the whole damn thing and all that, to the critical. In the critical, we sort it all out and then have kind of a celebration of how smart we are. And then when we move beyond that, to the postcritical, we say this is the lively word of God. My teacher, James Muilenburg, who I mentioned earlier and who lectured in your church back in 1961, taught Old Testament to seminarians at Union Theological Seminary. His first assignment was always to parse out the different layers or sources that, according to Julius Wellhausen's classic formulation of the Documentary Hypothesis, represent different social-historical contexts that were later edited together to form the Torah or Pentateuch. And it got to be the custom at Union that, on the day when those papers were due, the students all lined up with their papers and they walked in, chanting, "Moses wrote the whole damn thing! Moses wrote the whole damn thing!" And of course he loved it!

**CRB:** So we still have to know that stuff. It is important to understand, for example, that the Torah comprises different literary sources from different times and places that have been edited together into a more or less final form. We need to move beyond the precritical phase— "Moses wrote the whole damn thing!"—to the critical. But we should not stop there.

**WB:** That's right. We don't have to know every detail of the Documentary Hypothesis and other critical theories concerning the composition of the biblical canon, but we have to be aware of how complicated it all is, that it didn't just drop down from the sky. But don't stop there.

# THIS PARTICULAR
# MANIFESTATION OF HOLINESS
## *What Makes the Bible So Special?*

**CRB:** What about the use of Scripture in worship?

**WB:** Well I'm for it! We ought to be reflecting on this text that is our peculiar text that nobody else is reflecting on when we worship. One of the critiques of the United Church of Christ, which is my denomination, is that you would think that the *New York Times* is its canonical text and not the Bible. So we need to see that our capacity for theological imagination really depends on continuing to be nurtured and confronted by the irascible quality of this text. And over the long history of the church, we have tried many substitutes. Medieval Catholicism sort of thought that Aristotle was a better text, and of late we have thought that Freud or Marx might be a better text. We need to read all those texts very carefully and thoughtfully, but none of them is our text.

**CRB:** One might ask, but why does this particular text deserve our attention more than any other? What makes the Bible so special and worthy of such close and careful work? To put it in more theological terms, we might ask about things like inspiration or "the authority of Scriptures" or "special revelation." But seriously, why should this text be given such special treatment? What warrants that kind of attention by us?

**WB:** It gives a script for articulating our life from the bottom up in terms of dialogical fidelity. And there aren't any other scripts that do that, not any that I know about. The dialogical part seems to me to be really important, but of course that requires a certain understanding of the God of the Bible as a dialogical character, that is, a character that takes on life and form in dialogical relationship with others. I may be wrong about this, but I don't think anybody in fact lives an ad hoc life. I think everybody has some kind of metanarrative or script that they live by, usually one that they don't remember choosing. The Bible is an available metanarrative that offers a way of life that is not offered in any other metanarrative.

---

If I had to give a theological answer about why the Bible's important, it's because it is the only available testimony to this particular manifestation of holiness.

---

I myself have concluded that formal discussions about "inspiration" and "special revelation" and all that get us absolutely nowhere. I can affirm all that, but it does not help. Long ago, when I was young (very long ago), in an annual meeting of the Society of Biblical Literature at Vanderbilt, we had a panel on the authority of Scripture. The Roman Catholic on the panel went through all the Vatican announcements. Then the Protestant scholar did a history of Jerome and a history of Luther and so on. Finally the Jew, the late great Samuel Sandmel, a liberal, got up and said, "We love these books," and then sat back down. I don't know if I can go any further than that.

For me personally, and professionally, it's a given. And so I'm going to go from there. It's a little bit like, you didn't choose your parents. They came with your life. We didn't really choose this book. If we had chosen the book, we could've chosen a better book. But it's the one we got. And we cannot depart from it without ceasing to be who we are. This irascible character of God is not given to us anywhere else. So it's not just the book that we hold on to. It's the character that's rendered in the book who is endlessly fascinating and without whom we cannot live. If I had to give a theological answer about why the Bible is important, it's because it is the only available testimony to this particular manifestation of holiness.

# DISJUNCTIVE, CONTRADICTORY, HYPERBOLIC, IRONIC
## *Recovering Jewish Modes of Interpretation*

**CRB:** I'm not thrilled with labels like "liberal," "conserva-tive," "progressive," "evangelical," "fundamentalist," and so on. But indulge me the shorthand for a minute. Although I was raised in a nonreligious family and grew up going to a Pentecostal church on my own, I am now a pastor in a church that likes to describe itself as pro-gressive but would probably be labeled liberal by most conservative Christians. For the sake of convenience, I usually describe myself that way too, although I still feel a great love for and debt to my Pentecostal roots. At any rate, in my church context of progressive or liberal Christianity, many are asking why the Bible should mat-ter for us today. What is its relevance? How do we claim it, or rather reclaim it? How do we stop apologizing for it? We say in our creeds and confessions that it's author-itative for life and faith. But I think many people of faith are honestly not sure what that means or how to make it meaningful. How do you talk to folks like us about why the Bible matters today?

**WB:** I think the relevance of the Bible is that the God of the gospel is embedded in the text, and you cannot get to that God in a thoughtful, sustained way if you do not pay attention to the text in which this God is embedded.

This God is a character in a narratives and poetry of the Bible, and so you have to study those texts as such. Perhaps the best way to get over our embarrassment is just to commit a great act of chutzpah and say, as in the old hymn, "This is my story, this is my song." And just do it. That's what I think.

**CRB:** I always like it when you conclude a point with, "That's what I think." Still, your approach may be easier said than done for many. What do you think is our resistance to adopting what you describe as more Jewish modes? What is the Christian resistance? We talked earlier about all the "Bible baggage" many of us are carrying around.

**WB:** I think our resistance stems from the fact that we've largely cast the Bible in categories of Greek philosophy, which, compared to Jewish tradition, is quite static. And because of Christian triumphalism, we have wanted to make universal statements, which claim to be true everywhere and always, rather than making confessional statements, which say, this is our perception of reality, here and now. A confessional statement is not a description of reality that everyone can embrace. It is a taking of sides on big, deep issues and a refusing to be evenhanded about it.

Part of what needs to happen in the church, I think, is to recover Jewish modes of perception and articulation over against the Hellenistic modes that dominate Christian ways of reading and thinking about the Bible. These Hellenistic modes, which the modern West has inherited, lead us to believe that everything has to fit together into a single, totalizing, transcendent truth, without contradiction.

**CRB:** Omniscient, omnipotent, omnipresent . . . all those.

**WB:** That's right. We Christians are schooled in that mode. When I say we need to recover Jewish modes, I mean modes that are disjunctive and contradictory and hyperbolic and ironic—all the stuff that does not fit our usual ways of doing things, and that certainly does not fit our usual ways of doing faith. So that's very challenging.

But if we can give up the static qualities of Greek philosophy, if we can give up the seduction of speaking universalisms, then we can have the freedom of our own confessional practice. And here we can learn from Jewish modes. Compared to static universalism, Jewish tradition is essentially dialogical, relational, and interactive, as we can see particularly in the work of Martin Buber and Emmanuel Levinas. And that means that there is a huge resistance within this tradition to systemization. So by and large, rabbinic tradition is not in the business of systemizing Jewish faith. What rabbis do is take a text at a time and read it, and then they read another text, and then they read another text, and they have no obligation to make it all fit together. That's the pivot point: the text offers an open-ended, relational, dramatic articulation that resists universalism and essentialism.

I reviewed a book some time ago by Steven Gimbel called *Einstein's Jewish Science* (2012) in which he showed that, because Einstein's theory of relativity opposed the static categories of German national socialism, they labeled his research Jewish by way of dismissing it. I know nothing about relativity or Einstein, but while reading the book, it occurred to me that Einstein's theory of relativity is utterly Jewish because what Einstein saw was that reality is a dynamism of many interrelated moving parts that cannot be settled into a static formulation. It seems to me that, in theological terms, relativity means that every part of reality is relative to other parts, including God. So God's relativity to Israel means that the way Israel conducts itself impacts who God is able to be that day. And that certainly flies in the face of theological categories like omniscience, omnipresence, and so on. I really think that is so elemental to biblical tradition, and I think most church people haven't a clue about it.

**CRB:** How do you find Christian people react to this kind of relational, disjunctive, contradictory, hyperbolic, and ironic mode of biblical engagement? You keep teaching and preaching about this disjunctiveness in the Bible—and in the God of the Bible.

**WB:** What I try to do is to focus on the immediate specificity of the text and to see how the words produce the character of God, and then if somebody doesn't like that, or cannot quite get to it, they don't have to be mad at me; they just have to look at that text. So I think that when you do that, very many people are surprised. Some people are upset.

I was recently doing something like this at the National Cathedral with the dean before the service on Sunday morning. He was pressing me about my understanding

---

I think people are fascinated by what they find in the text. I think they are invited to press further. I think we are intimidated by it, and even shocked. I think it creates a moment in which something new can happen, if we have the courage and the wits to allow it.

of God, to the point where I finally articulated my current conviction about God and violence: that God in the Bible is in recovery. And this so upset the dean that he almost terminated the conversation. He didn't know what the next question could be.

So I think people are fascinated by what they find in the text. I think they are invited to press further. I think we are intimidated by it, and even shocked. I think it creates a moment in which something new can happen, if we have the courage and the wits to allow it. Of course there are always some people who recognize that it entails a large undoing of everything they had thought, and the way they had organized their faith, and they don't want to go there. But that's not my primary experience.

There is no doubt that many people resonate with such an articulation when they can be freed from conventional unexamined assumptions that are often fostered by the church. The reason we resonate is because we know, when we are honest, that our own lives are like that—marked by disjunction, contradiction, and irony, the stuff that requires hyperbole for full articulation.

# WHAT KIND OF WORLD
DO YOU WANT?

*Acts of Imagination*

**CRB:** Part of what you're beginning to touch on here is what you have described as the world-making power of language, that speech leads reality. Can you unpack that?

**WB:** I think that crafted, artistic speech is not descriptive but imaginative. It is an act of imagination that says, "I am going to sketch out a world for you in what I am about to say, and you entertain this alternative picture of reality for a little while and see how that feels to you."

After a while, we who live in and are oriented to that alternative world will use shorthand, to allude to parts of it, because we no longer have to sketch it all the way out. So on the seven Sundays of the season of Easter, when the minister says, "Christ is risen!" and the congregation responds, "He is risen indeed!" that is a performative act of the whole Easter narrative, proclaiming that the power of the Roman Empire has failed. Unfortunately, most church people don't know that that's what they are saying when they say it. But that little cliché is very thick. It is a declaration that we live in a world where the visible power of the empire, any empire, is fake—a source of "fake news"!

What we have to recognize is that most of the "real world" that we take for granted is also an act of rhetoric. This is why teaching the humanities is so important. The humanities really consist of the long record of world construction by humans. Nobody knew that the world was organized into eternal forms and ideas until Plato said it. Adam Smith created a world with his rhetoric of capitalism. Karl Marx created a world of alternative economic possibility with his passionate writing. And so on. Any world that can be knowingly embraced and transmitted to the next generation has to be brought to speech. Speech shapes reality into a livable possibility.

And when you do world construction, people who are on the receiving end of that communication can decide whether or not they are going to live in that world, which of course is what happens in a family. Parents do world construction: "This is how we do it." And then kids arrive at a certain age and say, "That's not the world I want to live in anymore." Except on Christmas Eve or Easter, they are very glad to return to that familiar world.

So I think we move in and out of worlds. And what has happened to the church, particularly the liberal church, is that we have been rhetorically constructing a world that is so like the dominant world that people can't even tell the difference. Liberals have just echoed culture. On the other hand, conservatives have compartmentalized, so they create a little bitty alternative world that doesn't relate to anything. This leaves us undisturbed in the dominant world, which is grounded in etiologies that are alien to the gospel. The whole reason to be an opinion maker, pastor, teacher, journalist, is to shape an imagined world that evokes certain kinds of policies and certain kinds of conduct. Ronald Reagan was a master at creating a world that legitimated some very bad policies. He loved to tell stories about welfare queens that had very little connection to reality, but his stories created a world from which policies emerged.

# IN, WITH, AND UNDER

## The God of the Text

**CRB:** So the church's world-shaping rhetoric emerges from and in relation with the biblical text. And for you, that includes our language about God. Earlier in our conversation, you said you try to "focus on the immediate specificity of the text and to see how the words *produce* the character of God." You say "produce," not "reflect" or "represent" what is already present before and outside the text?

**WB:** That's right. Maybe better "generate" than "produce." God is situated in these biblical patterns of rhetoric, without which you cannot have this God. Which, as you know, is why I insist in my *Theology of the Old Testament* that God exists in this text and "nowhere else."

**CRB:** Ok, let's go there. Here's what you write:

> God is given to us (and exists as God "exists") only by the dangerous practices of rhetoric. Therefore in doing Old Testament theology we must be careful not to import essentialist claims that are not authorized by this particular and peculiar rhetoric. *I shall insist, as consistently as I can, that the God of Old Testament theology as such lives in, with, and under the rhetorical enterprise of this text, and nowhere else and in no other way.*

Please say more. I often wonder if very many people who say they love your work really can hear that. It's quite radical. I imagine a lot of people who've read or heard you make this point say, "Well, he doesn't really mean that. He doesn't really mean 'nowhere else' . . . There would still be this God even if we didn't have this text. God must ultimately transcend this rhetoric."

**WB:** I am aware of that opinion. But I do not think that *this God* can transcend *this text*. As soon as we look elsewhere for this God, the radical relationality of this God—filled with disjunction, holiness, and fidelity—is compromised. This God, I suggest, stays "on script." This script is the natural habitat of this God.

It is radical because the Bible is radical. I think that any dimension of God that you might want to celebrate—holiness, mercy, compassion, whatever—this is language that is given to us in what we call a revelation. This language has somehow been disclosed to us. When we are baptized and when we sign on with this casting of reality, we affirm that this is an adequate, authentic world in which we are willing and able to live, and it is in that world, in these texts, that the mercy and justice and righteousness—the fidelity of God—is most elementally enacted.

We could think, for example, of the Exodus narrative as a kind of script that is waiting to be reperformed—in a Passover Seder meal, for example. It's analogous in some ways to a score by Beethoven. Every time an orchestra plays it, that orchestra reperforms the script in a new way. The script puts all kinds of restraints on the performers, but it also allows huge freedom for the performers. It is that delicate balance between restraint and freedom, I think, that is the world in which we live. It's not entirely coherent.

That's really what Jesus was doing in his parables as well. He was world constructing. Take the phrase with which Jesus introduces his parables: "the kingdom of God is like," or in Matthew "the kingdom of heaven is like." The alternative world of the gospel is "like." Imagine, for example, a world in which the wayward son is welcomed home. The great homiletics professor Fred Craddock said that he once got invited, on the spur of the moment, to teach a Sunday school class, so he did the parable of the wayward or prodigal son. Just for fun, he said, "When the younger son came home, the father said, 'You get on down to the barn and work. I am not glad to see you.'" And a voice in the back of the Sunday school room said, "That's what he should have said." The parable is an alternative world to the one that *should* have happened—and might yet happen. The parable is waiting to be enacted!

Jesus's parables are filled with outrageous scenarios that challenge our accepted characterization of the world . . . a wayward child who doesn't get what he deserves, getting paid when you show up at the ninth hour just as much as others got paid for working the whole day, and so on. They are alternative worlds, mandating and liberating us to live a different kind of life. The problem for the church is that we get an hour a week with people who are bombarded with all of these other world constructions all week. We really don't stand a chance. And I suppose in Jesus' time, the alternative world of the gospel was competing against a combination of the narrative of the Roman Empire and the colluding Jewish leadership, and he got barely a handful of converts out of it.

So, yes, I believe it, "that the God of Old Testament theology as such lives in, with, and under the rhetorical enterprise of this text, and nowhere else and in no other way." Of course it's complex. But I think for any faith claim to be transmitted, it cannot be free of speech. It is through speech. And if it's through speech, then what you get out of this speech in contrast to that speech makes a difference. Therefore, we are committed to certain images and cadences that we believe are truthful and adequate. I don't think we are in the business of declaring all other faith speech as untrue; that's just not what we are up to. Instead we say, if you come here, you may expect this talk. In the ordination process, through which someone becomes an ordained minister or priest or rabbi or imam, the church wants to know that you can talk the way "we" talk.

**CRB:** Your use of "in, with, and under" in that passage brings to mind the familiar Lutheran belief that Christ's presence is available "in, with, and under" the consecrated bread and wine of the Eucharist. Do you think there is something incarnational going on in the biblical text that makes this God available?

**WB:** I hadn't really thought about that when I used the phrase, and I'm not sure what all that signifies, but yes, I think that I do mean it that way. Yes.

**CRB:** So could we say that doing biblical theology via close reading is in some sense sacramental?

**WB:** That's exactly right. And for Protestants, who are not so hot on the Eucharist, to see the text work as sacramental is really important.

# DIVINE IRASCIBILITY
*An Astonishing and Scandalous God*

**CRB:** At the same time, the God that is "generated" or "made available" through this text work can confront orthodox Christian theology in disturbing and fascinating ways (which I think is part of what makes this text work so interesting to many college students, religious and nonreligious and antireligious alike!).

One aspect of the God we discover here is what you call *irascibleness*, which I think means something like unpredictably quick-tempered or touchy. Earlier in our conversation, for example, you said that it was this "irascible character of God" in the Bible, which is " the only available testimony to this particular manifestation of holiness." Could you say more? I love the word irascible. I had to look it up.

**WB:** I think that this character in this text is capable of astonishing and scandalous and surprising actions, which keep the world open. If we inhale this testimony, it invites us to some irascibility as well, which means that we are not cookie-cutter creatures. Rather we are practitioners of huge freedom, with all the costs and privileges pertaining thereto. I think it's very hard for church people to entertain the irascible character of God.

In the lectionary that my church follows, we have been getting Genesis recently for the Old Testament readings. In *Jacob and the Divine Trickster* (2011), John E. Anderson argues that Jacob is both a shameless trickster and God's favorite in the stories about him in Genesis (chapters 25–36). More than the trickery of Jacob, Anderson shows that what is operating here is a "theology of deception"—that the Jacob stories are as much about God as trickster as they are about Jacob as trickster. The narrative suggests that the plot of the story is thick with the holy working of God, who is decisive for the story even if kept in the background. Of course, this articulation of God, who here is devious and against the grain of fairness or normal expectation, does not fit our common assumptions about God. But then, that is the work of the Bible: to show us continually the fresh freedom of God just when we think we have God all figured out. Jacob could not figure God out, but he relied on the passion of God for his own future.

**CRB:** Can you think of other biblical texts that reflect this theology of deception, in which God is a trickster?

**WB:** In 1 Samuel 16, when God dispatches Samuel to anoint David as king of Israel instead of Saul, Samuel is afraid to go. So God says, "Well, just lie a little. Tell him you've come to offer a sacrifice." And then in 1 Kings 22, God allows a lying spirit to enter into all the prophets so that they encourage the king of Israel to go into battle, assuring him of victory, when in fact God had decreed disaster for him and his armies. And I suppose in some ways you could say that the entire book of Job is about a God who does not operate according to theological protocol.

I suppose you could also say that the Jesus parables witness to this trickster God, because there is often a surprising twist, in which God doesn't act according to our expectations of the way God should act.

**CRB:** Where does the fault lie in our avoidance of this biblical God? Is it that laypeople won't tolerate it because it doesn't fit with our protocols, with what we expect theologically of the Bible—that it be changeless, omniscient, omnipresent, and so on? Or do clergy turn away as well?

**WB:** I think it's all that. I also think that the historical-critical approach to biblical studies in seminaries has explained everything away by contextualizing stories like those of God as trickster in earlier, less enlightened perspectives, as primitive folklore. I discovered that much too late for my own work. I think on all fronts what turns us away from taking this biblical rhetoric seriously is an effort to domesticate God in order to fit Enlightenment rationality. The God of Enlightenment rationality cannot do anything. So the great embarrassment for liberals is that God should have agency. And conservatives don't really believe in the agency of God, either; they believe in a scholastic formula for God, but it's all static and closed.

I suppose you could also say that the Jesus parables witness to this trickster God, because there is often a surprising twist in which God doesn't act according to our expectations of the way God should act.

**CRB:** Process theology, it seems to me, is a reaction against that static language—to get outside all of the "omni" words, and to reintroduce dynamism and change into our understanding of God. But you would argue it is doing something very different from what you are doing in your biblical theology, because it also depersonalizes God. Am I getting that right?

**WB:** I think that's right. Because all of our great biblical terms of faith—mercy, compassion, love, forgiveness—are interpersonal words. They're not just stuff in the sky. You cannot be forgiven unless there is a forgiver, and so on. Of course, you don't get any of that kind of dynamism in process theology, which is more philosophical, because it's too embarrassed by such interpersonal theological language. There is no "agent" in process theology.

Most of us want to cast theology in Newtonian terms, that is, according to fixed laws within a static, closed system. I think that the Newtonian static casting of biblical theology is what led to process theology. But we wouldn't have needed process theology if we had in the first place understood that biblical theology is essentially dialogic and relational. Process theology, as I understand it, is an attempt to recover all that relational stuff to God without the embarrassments of personality or agency. The biblical articulation of this is covenant. In the Bible, the covenant can be unilateral, enacted, and guaranteed by God; or it can be bilateral, depending on the fidelity of God's partner. It can be eternally durable, assured by God; or it can be conditional, and then terminated, and perhaps remade in fresh fashion. All things are possible in a relational reality that is not governed by any predictable logic.

# GOD IN RECOVERY
## *The Bible and Violence*

**CRB:** Speaking of divine personality and agency—and also irascibility—you referred earlier to God and violence in the Bible and suggested that "God in the Bible is in recovery." That's provocative. Will you say more about that? Where and how do you see that happening in the text?

**WB:** Anyone who teaches the Old Testament is always getting asked about the violence of God in the Old Testament. Our usual way of answering that, which is a liberal way of answering it, is to say, "Well, the most violent parts are from the earliest J (Jahwist) source, which is a primitive projection of God. But the later D (Deuteronomist) source will be better if you just wait a little while. And then we'll get another layer, and it'll be alright."

I think that is too easy. So I want to say that these presentations of God's violence in the biblical text are not human projections but revelations of God. Well, what then? My thesis is that the God of the Old Testament—and into the New, really—is in recovery from having been an agent of violence. And everybody who is in recovery from time to time regresses. So God sometimes falls back into violence.

My thesis is that the God of the Old Testament—and into the New, really—is in recovery from having been an agent of violence. And everybody who is in recovery from time to time regresses. So God sometimes falls back into violence.

Now the lead text—and it may be betting too much on one text, but we will do that for the moment—is Hosea 11, which is an incredible text.

[1] When Israel was a child, I loved him,
    and out of Egypt I called my son.
[2] The more I called them,
    the more they went from me;
they kept sacrificing to the Baals,
    and offering incense to idols.

[3] Yet it was I who taught Ephraim to walk,
    I took them up in my arms;
    but they did not know that I healed them.
[4] I led them with cords of human kindness,
    with bands of love.
I was to them like those
    who lift infants to their cheeks.
    I bent down to them and fed them.

[5] They shall return to the land of Egypt,
    and Assyria shall be their king,
    because they have refused to return to me.
[6] The sword rages in their cities,
    it consumes their oracle-priests,
    and devours because of their schemes.

⁷ My people are bent on turning away from me.
    To the Most High they call,
        but he does not raise them up at all.

⁸ How can I give you up, Ephraim?
    How can I hand you over, O Israel?
How can I make you like Admah?
    How can I treat you like Zeboiim?
My heart recoils within me;
    my compassion grows warm and tender.
⁹ I will not execute my fierce anger;
    I will not again destroy Ephraim;
for I am God and no mortal,
    the Holy One in your midst,
        and I will not come in wrath. (Hosea 11:1–9)

In the first four verses, God says to Israel, "You know, when you were a little baby, I brought you out of Egypt, and I loved you, and I fed you, and I taught you how to walk, and I took care of you, and you were so cuddly, and I just adored you."

And then, by verse five, Israel has clearly become a teenager. God says, "Get the hell out of my house! I am done with you. I don't care if the Assyrians conquer you—that's okay with me! I'm done!"

Then, at the end of verse seven, there is a pause. As every parent of every teenager knows, it's a pause of self-reflection. Like, "What am I doing here?" The poet has God catch God's self mid-sentence in the tirade. God interrupts God!

And then, in verse eight, God says, "How can I give you up? How can I treat you like Sodom and Gomorrah? I don't want to be that kind of God! I'm not going to act that way." I think that, in verses 5 to 7, God is willing to allow violence against God's beloved people, because they made God so goddamned mad! And then, according to the poem, God comes to this self-aware moment and says, "That's not the real me!" I think that is the kind of self-discovery that goes on in a recovery program.

And there are other texts like that. There may not be enough of them. But there are some. So that's my way of thinking about that vis-à-vis the biblical text. Obviously, what that does, is it brings God into the covenantal transaction in ways that do not fit with the church legacy that God is omnipotent and omniscient and omnipresent and I don't know what-all. I just think the Bible is so much more interesting than that doctrinal tradition of the church.

**CRB:** How do people react to that kind of close reading when it leads to an image of God that is so far outside our doctrinal tradition of God as omni-everything, and also so challenging to our images of God as loving? Do you think people feel liberated taking the text so literally, even when it flies in the face of orthodoxy? Are they liberated by encountering such a provocative image of God right there in the Bible?

**WB:** I don't think they're necessarily converted. But I think most people at least want to sit there with it for a minute.

**CRB:** It resonates more with the human experience, I think, to have God be in the midst of all those different behaviors and emotions. And it reflects us because it's not neat and orderly. Our lives are not neat and orderly.

**WB:** That's right. You see, Freud's great insight (and Freud was Jewish and steeped in Hebrew biblical tradition) is that the human self is multilayered and conflicted. For all of Freud's resistance to Jewishness, his theory of psychoanalysis is thoroughly Jewish in the way that he understood that we are carriers of incredible complexity, and we have to process all that. All human selves are multilayered and conflicted.

So is the biblical text. Just think, for example, about the multiple layers or literary sources that were edited together to produce the Torah (J, E, D, and P in the now classic Documentary Hypothesis, alluded to earlier). They have distinct voices reflecting different theologies and different historical contexts. When those multiple, conflicting layers come together in the Torah, you have a biblical God that is multilayered and is conflicted. And we are made in the image of that God. And that certainly gets carried into the rest of the Old Testament, and into the New Testament. So the awareness of how God is in this testimony is always at the same time something of an act of self-discovery and self-awareness—about how I am in the world as well.

The same complexity is reflected in rabbinic engagement with Scripture, in which multiple readings of a particular text are offered side-by-side in commentary. Texts sanction no single reading even though a single settled reading is a great temptation among us Christians. It is a habit we have acquired from being so closely attached to the ways of empire. The God of covenant refuses all of our reductionisms.

# THE OFFENSE OF JESUS
*Death as the Seedbed of Life*

**CRB:** Let's talk about Jesus.

**WB:** Oh, sure. Just when we were having a good time.

**CRB:** When Tim and I were in our first semester at Columbia Theological Seminary, and you had just joined the faculty a year earlier, New Testament scholar Beverly Gaventa invited you to guest lecture in her introduction to the New Testament course. (Actually, it seemed like you were invited to guest lecture in just about every course we took during that first year—New Testament, church history, pastoral care, you name it!)

**WB:** You know why that probably happened? I was new at the seminary, as you said, and I think my colleagues were thinking, "I hear he's saying this stuff. I can't believe it, so I'm going to have him guest lecture in my class to see whether he's really saying it."

**CRB:** Perhaps! Or maybe they just wanted their attendance to go up that day! At any rate, there we were in our New Testament class with you guest lecturing. I can't remember on what text, but I think it was in Luke. And when you were finished with your lecture, one student raised his hand and asked, "But what about Jesus?" And you answered, tongue in cheek, "I'm not paid to talk about him."

**WB:** Did I say that?

**CRB:** Yes, you did! But you do talk about Jesus. So, what about Jesus? Much like when it comes to the Bible, we liberal-progressive types are sometimes embarrassed to talk about Jesus. How is Jesus faring in the church these days, and how are we in the mainline church engaging with Jesus?

**WB:** Many years ago, when I was on sabbatical in England, I heard this joke. One old British professor says to another, "Did you know that Professor Watson has published his autobiography?" The other asks, "Really? What did he call it?" And the first replies, "He called it *The Life of Jesus.*"

We are always refashioning Jesus in our own image, and every one of us does it. Liberals like me tend to accent the human liberationist Jesus, and more conservative people fall out on the other side of the equation and kind of remove Jesus from the fray of history. So I think the hardest theological thing to do in the church is the doctrinal formulation that Jesus is both truly God and truly human, and to hold together that mystery on which our well-being depends.

We struggle to let Jesus be Jesus' own authentic revolutionary self, and not to tone down Jesus to our mode. Calvin has this wonderful statement that I learned from my former colleague George Stroup. Calvin says, essentially, that Jesus is rendered in many different ways but always in the way that people in that context need to have Jesus rendered. So he's a savior, he's a liberator, he's a healer, he's a cleanser, he's a feeder. And our temptation is to reduce all that to one image that makes sense to me and my context rather than to let the church, in its great diversity, have Jesus in many ways. Which I assume is why we have four Gospels, because the four Gospels were addressed to different congregations who had different needs.

I now worship at an Episcopal church, and the only time I cringe is when, in the Episcopal liturgy, we say that eventually Jesus will bring all things in subjection under his rule. I understand why we say that, but we have to find a different way to say that; we cannot say that in a religiously pluralistic culture, where there are other legitimate faith claims. In the arena of interreligious exchanges, it seems to me, what we have to say is that we make a confession that Jesus is Lord, but that a confession is a different thing from a cosmic imposition, such as the lordship of Jesus over all. I think we have a great deal of homework to do about that.

---

We struggle to let Jesus be Jesus' own authentic revolutionary self, and not to tone down Jesus to our mode.

---

**CRB:** This is a tremendous challenge for the church today. As a community of faith, we proclaim Jesus' lordship. But that can sound imperialistic and triumphalist in the context of our larger religiously diverse society. Still, we cannot give up that faith-specific language within the community, or we lose who we are. We are nervous to even put Jesus, let alone the lordship of Jesus, in a mission statement, because it is so loaded and because we don't want to offend anyone. Because that imperial, triumphalist understanding of Christianity is still so prevalent and familiar to people, especially to non-Christians, we often find ourselves explaining, "I'm a Christian, but not *that* kind of Christian." We get nervous about being mistaken for that other kind of Christian who imagines it's all about subjecting the whole world, like it or not, to Christ's dominion and lordship. What do you say to us, who are so anxious to point out that we're not "those kind" of Christians?

**WB:** That reminds me of all these seminaries that the right wing has taken over in recent decades. People will say, "I went to Southern Baptist Theological Seminary in Louisville, *but* I was in there in 1973." Well, I suppose that we want our talk about Jesus to be congruent with our walk with Jesus, and for us that walk with Jesus has to do with generosity, forgiveness, hospitality, and neighborliness. And what we hope is that when we talk about Jesus, we have an opportunity to say, "the Jesus who I trust and worship is the one who authorizes me to live this kind of life." And then we must bring our own walk into congruity with our talk, an endless piece of work.

When you play the imperial Constantinian game of proclaiming the ultimate universal lordship of Christ, then it's easy to offend for what I think are misguided reasons. There is an offense in the Christian gospel, but it's not the offense of absolute power that statements like the one in my Episcopal liturgy about the universal lordship of Christ proclaim. The offense of the gospel, the offense of Jesus, is that death is the seedbed of life. It is the offense that Easter Sunday can only come out of Good Friday. So in 1 Corinthians, when Paul says that the cross is a scandal to Greeks and a stumbling block to Jews, that's what he's talking about. The offense is a different offense than we imagine. It's not about lordship, but suffering and death. It's the offense that Friedrich Nietzsche spotted when he said that Christianity is faith for weak people. But it is a faith for weak people that subverts all worldly claims to power. That's the offense.

I think what we have to do, wherever we have opportunity, is to do interpretation that exposes those fraudulent articulations of Jesus that are everywhere around us in our society. It is the case that this right-wing character of Jesus focuses on about ten carefully selected biblical texts, and we have to make the case that there is a lot of other important stuff here, and you cannot reduce it that way. Wherever we can, we have to do a frontal job about that, to critique them from the ground up. I think of Mel Gibson's movie (*The Passion of the Christ*) and all his craziness. But I also think that we have to critique the Jesus Seminar, which really wants to produce a very thin Jesus. I am committed to the Jesus that I think is the faithful interpretive tradition in the church. We have to do a better job, not only of letting other people know about that, but also of understanding that ourselves. If we do not, then we end up in a very defensive posture, and we don't need to be defensive. When we are intellectually lazy, we will undoubtedly fall into cultural stereotypes, and that is what has happened to us.

**CRB:** In 2017, you were part of a group of American theologians and pastors who wrote a public declaration: "Reclaiming Jesus: A Confession of Faith in a Time of Crisis" (reclaimingjesus.org). It begins, "We are living through perilous and polarizing times as a nation, with a dangerous crisis of moral and political leadership at the highest levels of our government and in our churches. We believe the soul of the nation and the integrity of faith are now at stake." It then offers six confessional statements concerning what "we believe" and what we therefore reject. First, "we believe" that everyone is created in God's image, and "therefore, we reject" nationalism. Second, "we believe" we are one body in Christ, and "therefore, we reject" misogyny, sexual harassment, and any other form of oppression against anyone. Third, "we believe" that how we treat the most vulnerable in society is how we treat Christ, and "therefore, we reject" political language and policies that "debase and abandon" them. Fourth, "we believe" that truthfulness is "morally central" to personal and public life, and "therefore, we reject" the lying and incivility that is increasingly in our civil life. Fifth, "we believe" that Christ models servanthood rather than domination, and "therefore, we reject" any form of authoritarian political rule. Sixth, "we believe" Jesus when he tells Christians to go to all nations and make disciples, and "therefore, we reject" American exceptionalism and "America first" ideology as a "theological heresy." Please say more about your work on this document.

**WB:** We came together to write "Reclaiming Jesus" because of our shared sense that this is a "Bonhoeffer moment" in our society. As you may know, Dietrich Bonhoeffer was a leading church resister to Nazism in Germany when he, along with other German church pastors and members, judged that the movement of Hitler was a profound and dangerous contradiction to the truth and rule of Christ in the world. Out of that readiness to resist came the Barmen Declaration in 1934. That church declaration asserted, in six statements, that the rule of Nazism must be resisted and refused by serious Christians who confessed the rule of Christ. Each of these six statements in the declaration included both a positive claim for Christ and a negative critique of Nazism.

Our declaration, "Reclaiming Jesus," is intentionally patterned after the Barman Declaration because we judge that the dominant ordering of our society is now a profound contradiction to the rule of Christ and that a bold assertion now is required of us so that our confession of Christ may have sociopolitical reality. In making this declaration it is our hope and expectation that it will be shared with and affirmed by many church pastors and members in recognition of our shared baptismal faith that summons us to resistance.

# DOCTRINAL OVERLAYS

*From Jesus in the Gospels to Jesus in the Trinity*

**CRB:** You say that a central task for us as Christians today is to "do interpretation that exposes those fraudulent articulations of Jesus that are everywhere around us in our society." What does that work look like, on the ground, in our work with the biblical texts?

**WB:** I think we have such traditional doctrinal overlays on the Jesus of the Gospels. We'd do well to read more biblical texts. What the church wants to confess about Jesus in the doctrine of the Trinity, for example, is inchoate in the Gospel narratives. But as an exegete, I don't want to spend too much time on that doctrinal overlay because what the earliest followers of Jesus discovered, without having read any of the creeds, was that "This is the guy. This is the guy who is the clue to creation." What the church in the third and fourth centuries then did was to develop formulas, like the doctrine of the Trinity in the Nicene Creed, to try to protect that claim. And since then I think we have too often been wrapped up in defending the formulas rather than paying attention to what the formulas meant to articulate. So when the writer of Colossians says, "In him all things hold together," well, that seems to say that Jesus really is the creator, one with the Father, and all that we get in the creedal formulas. But that's not really what that phrase says. It's poetic, and it says he's the glue, and life makes sense when you draw close to his life and his ministry and his summons.

**CRB:** Earlier, when we were focused on the Old Testament, you talked about a kind of "disjunctiveness" that you find operating there, one that testifies to an astonishing and sometimes upsetting irascibility in the personality and agency of God. Do you see that same kind of disjunctiveness in the Gospels, and, if so, what does that open up for us about the character of Jesus?

**WB:** The place where I would start is the parable that he teaches his disciples in Luke 18. He is teaching them how to "pray always and not to lose heart," and he tells a story of a nagging widow. We call her the "importunate" or "persistent" widow because it sounds more polite than "nagging." But she wasn't being polite. She wanted justice from the judge, who feared neither God nor man. And she kept after him until he was so provoked that he just gave in and gave her justice. Then Jesus says to his disciples, if even this unjust judge will eventually give in to such nagging, "will not God grant justice to his chosen ones who cry to him day and night?" He doesn't say, "Pray like that and you will always get what you want." I think what Jesus is saying is: live a dialogical life and you will continue to be energized; you will not lose heart.

So I think you can move in a lot of directions about Jesus. His parables are mostly interactive and relational. I think he is basically resistant to frozen, static categories. He wants to open it all up, which of course is what made him a threat to the Jewish establishment and what made him a threat to the Roman establishment. Establishment power cannot tolerate that kind of dialogic stuff because it is inherently subversive. So that's how I see it working in the New Testament.

**CRB:** Do you have a favorite Gospel text for getting at this kind of ground-up testimony about Jesus?

**WB:** One of my favorites is Luke 7, where John the Baptist is in prison and he sends two of his disciples to Jesus to ask if he's the messiah they've been waiting for.

**CRB:** Now I remember: that was the text you were lecturing on in Professor Gaventa's class.

**WB:** That's probably right. I do love this text. So John asks, through his disciples, "Are you the one who is to come, or are we to wait for another?" And Jesus says, in so many words, "The creeds haven't been written yet, so I don't know." But he says, "Go and tell John what you have seen and heard: the blind receive their sight, the lame walk, the lepers are cleansed, the deaf hear, the dead are raised, the poor have good news brought to them." In other words, "Go tell John that everywhere I go stuff happens, everywhere I go the lame walk, lepers are cleansed, the poor rejoice and the dead are raised, and John can draw his own conclusion." So that's testimony that everywhere the person of Jesus went, the power of God was present in explicable form.

I personally find that narrative rendering much more helpful than to say, as I do every Sunday in the Episcopal church, "God from God, light from light, true God from true God." Because I can say all that, and I don't mind affirming that, but I don't find that enlivening the way I am energized by the actual text that bears primary witness to what the early church experienced with him.

So the church has to be bilingual. We have to preserve these classic formulas of the creeds about the Trinity and all of that, but we also have to think about Jesus like we're teaching these stories to a six-year-old. A six-year-old does not need to know about the three persons of the Trinity in one substance. A six-year-old needs to know that wherever Jesus shows up, things are changed for the better.

**CRB:** I heard a story about a new members class at a big mainline church. The pastor who was leading the class asked everyone to share why they had decided to join that church. Some said the children's program, some said the music program, some liked the preaching. Those kinds of things. And then one gentleman said, "Because my life has been changed here. I have been transformed in encountering Jesus here." It stunned the group to silence. I think many who might have mentioned the children's program or the music might have also had that kind of experience. But many of us are uncomfortable talking that way. It's so vulnerable.

**WB:** That's right. We all either have stories of transformation to tell or have yearnings that we may yet be transformed. Or, more likely, we have both.

# ARTICULATING AN ALTERNATE WORLD

*Clergy Work as a Life-and-Death Matter*

**CRB:** You have been "retired" from your faculty role at Columbia Theological Seminary for almost fifteen years. Your courses were pretty exclusively focused on the Old Testament while there. If you were back in the classroom as a full-time seminary professor, are there subjects that you would want to teach today that you weren't able to teach back then?

**WB:** There once was a New Testament professor who invested his working life in a close study of the dative and accusative endings of Greek nouns. He was asked, after fifty years, if he would do it all over again and spend his life in that way. He said, "Indeed not; I would focus exclusively on the dative!"

What I would really want to do now is to teach active clergy, after they've graduated from seminary and are working as full-time pastors. Because clergy have real questions in front of them that seminarians can't possibly have yet. What I would want to teach clergy is that this work that they do really is a life-and-death matter. It is about the public articulation of an alternate world, and there is nothing more important. I don't think seminarians are ready for that.

**CRB:** I remember when you preached at a recent Festival of Homiletics in Denver, you looked up from your manuscript, peered at us over those reading glasses of yours, and said, very gravely, that what we are doing is about life and death. I don't know if you used the word "fascist," but we all had the sense that that is potentially what we are facing, the rise of fascism, in the United States and around the world. It's that serious. I remember sitting up, and I think most of us in that room sat up. Like, oh that's right, we're not trying to just make people feel better. We are, as you say, trying to articulate an alternate world, and that alternate world is really the antithesis of fascism. It was very sobering, and also empowering, to imagine that what we do as preachers and pastors could have that kind of power.

**WB:** That's exactly right. I do think that the circumstance we are in—Donald Trump didn't create it, but he's a nice metaphor for it—is pressing people of faith back to basics, back behind the clichés, to ask the question, "What is this stuff really about?" Most wouldn't be able to articulate it, but what they sense is that the dominant identities given us in our culture have failed. People know that. So that is a very hopeful sign.

I heard a wonderful story about Martin Niemöller recently. You know, he was part of the Confessing Church, a movement in Germany opposing the Nazi regime's efforts to unify all Protestants under a fascist Reich Church. Hitler had just come to power, and Niemöller was included in a church delegation that was invited to meet with him. Niemöller was very young and uncredentialed at the time, so he was sitting in the very back of the room, mostly just watching. When it was over he went home, and his wife asked him, "What did you learn today?" And he said, "I learned that Herr Hitler is very frightened."

**CRB:** There's empire-threatening power in what we do. That's so important to remember. Thank you for calling us out about that. So what does this life-and-death pastoral work look like on the ground? Can you unpack the tasks that are involved?

**WB:** I think the first pastoral task, the first *critical* pastoral task, is to help people become aware that we live in a constructed world. And the second task is to help them see that that constructed world, which wants us to believe it is the only possible reality, is inadequate. And finally, we need to help them entertain the alternate world of the gospel and to perform it in our common public life.

That first step is so difficult. It is almost impossible for any of us to imagine life outside of that constructed world, because we are so tenured in the knowledge system. But the amazing thing is that every time the people of God meet for worship and study, that is what we are doing. For a minister to get up and say, on each of the seven Sundays of the Easter season, "Christ has risen!" and for the congregation to say, "He is risen indeed!" is to make an inflammatory countercultural affirmation. And you can see that it is inflammatory. During Easter season we read a lot from the book of Acts, about the early Jesus movement after the resurrection. You can see how inflammatory the movement is because every time they say, "Christ has risen," they got hauled into court, which represented the empire of technological military consumerism. The Roman authorities recognized that the declaration of the resurrection of Jesus is the most dangerous truth you can spout in the empire. And the amazing thing, you know, is that we still gather regularly to enact that. It's astonishing. It is still dangerous; it is still urgent!

I help edit the *Journal of Preachers* with my former colleague Erskine Clarke. He really decides everything and does all the editing, but I offer input. So we were busy collecting Easter sermons, and I said to Erskine, "We need to get some Easter sermons that bear public witness about the resurrection." But that's not the kind of sermons we get. And I understand why. It is so difficult. But it is important.

---

I think the first pastoral task, the first critical pastoral task, is to help people become aware that we live in a constructed world. And the second task is to help them see that that constructed world, which wants us to believe it is the only possible reality, is inadequate.

---

**CRB:** What do you get?

**WB:** Well, you get pastoral tales of individual people finding hope for their life. And I don't minimize that. I think the reason that the public dimension of the pastor's work in articulating an alternate world is so important is that there's nobody else left to do it. And if the church defaults, we are that much worse off. That's what I think. I think there is a lot of preliminary work to do in seminary before you can master that public dimension, but it's obviously a different enterprise. And you really have to be working on the ground to learn it.

The problem is that for people to understand that about "Christ is risen," you have to do so much teaching in order for them to have any frame of reference. You cannot understand how revolutionary it is if you're not fully aware of the dominant version that it threatens. And the dominant version always wants to keep its identity undisclosed and hidden. We don't want people to see that the ideology of military consumerism, or whatever else, is a construct. It just feels like the truth—or, as Stephen Colbert would say, it feels like "truthiness."

# FUNDING THE ELEMENTS
# OF IMAGINATION
## *Subversive Preaching*

**CRB:** How do you prepare to preach? What is your planning and writing process? How do you get from text to kerygma, or proclamation?

**WB:** When I was learning to preach, I was taught to make an outline, which I still do. I don't use many sermon illustrations, because the text itself is the illustration of the gospel. I try to stay pretty close to the text, to let the moves that are being made in the text determine the shape of what becomes a rough outline. Then I try to maximize what the beginning of the text is, and then the middle of the text, and then the end of the text. I suspect it doesn't happen very often, but what I wish to have happen is that people will go out of this place with another text in their repertoire.

I don't know how it would work if I were a pastor who had to preach every Sunday to the same congregation. But I generally preach to people whom I don't know, because I'm on the road, and so I stay very close to the text on the bet that, even though I don't know the people in this or that church, we are all struggling with the same things. Everybody is starting with the same stuff, and in one way or another, these texts make contact with that stuff, or we wouldn't keep coming back to them.

**CRB:** Frederick Buechner said that our deepest secrets are also the most universal.

**WB:** Yes, yes. I'm not much on preaching that tries to push for a behavioral outcome based on my latest particular pet project. I don't think it does any good. Since I sit at my desk all day and rarely interact with anybody, I don't have any sermon illustrations available. So I don't use any of those. I try to do contemporary connections only by way of throwaway lines. I don't want to try to be too relevant, because I want people in the congregation to do the work of relevance, and people have to decide for themselves what is relevant. What I want to do is to enrich and fund the elements of imagination that are available for people to process their life.

---

I want people in the congregation to do the work of relevance, and people have to decide for themselves what is relevant. What I want to do is to enrich and fund the elements of imagination that are available for people to process their life.

---

**CRB:** You also say that preaching is, or should be, a subversive act.

**WB:** Yes it is. The way I play with that is if you take the word "subversive" and turn it into a noun, you get "subversion," that is, sub-version. Preaching, at its best, is subversive because it offers a *subversion* of reality that contradicts the dominant version. Do you know the work of the anthropologist James C. Scott? I highly recommend two of his books in particular: *Weapons of the Weak* (1985) and *Domination and the Arts of Resistance* (1990). He did research in Malaysia on how peasants maintain their lives and dignity in a very authoritarian context without getting shot or imprisoned—so "weapons of the weak." His programmatic phrase is "hidden transcripts," which refers to the words and stories and images that peasants keep hidden from the masters, which of course is what African Americans have done throughout the history of slavery and beyond. I think the church is, at its best, a practice of hidden transcripts. And when you value and sustain those transcripts—those words and stories and images that offer a subversion of reality—they help you see that the public transcript of the dominant class is a fraud.

My most recent way of trying to get at subversiveness of preaching is that it is, or can be, an act of imaging the world as though God were a real character and an active agent. The dominant world doesn't mind having a God, but not a real character and not an active agent. Because if the world is indwelled by an active God or a real agent, then the two prophetic themes of judgment and salvation are important topics of our lives. If God is a real agent, the world is under judgment for the way we have organized social power. And if God is a real agent, there are good futures beyond the gift of the dominant narrative, which means there is hope for poor and disenfranchised people. But if you eliminate the notion that we are accountable for the mess we have made, if you eliminate God's judgment, and if you eliminate God's future, then we end in despair. What we get is an unlivable world, which is roughly what we are making.

So I'm inclined to let people have texts, like Jeremiah 5:26–29, which seems like an easy access point where God says, about the wicked,

For scoundrels are found among my people;
    they take over the goods of others.
Like fowlers they set a trap;
    they catch human beings.
Like a cage full of birds,
    their houses are full of treachery;
therefore they have become great and rich,
    they have grown fat and sleek.
They know no limits in deeds of wickedness;
    they do not judge with justice
the cause of the orphan, to make it prosper,
    and they do not defend the rights of the needy.
Shall I not punish them for these things?
                      says the LORD,
    and shall I not bring retribution
    on a nation such as this?

So God says that the wicked are like treacherous birders who catch the poor in a cage, and then he goes on to say you have not honored the cause of the orphans and the needy. Should I not punish you? Well, the congregation will have to answer that. The question of punishment does not come up unless there is a God involved here. I don't know what I would do if I had to preach every Sunday, but I really think that we have to let the text do some of the work. Say, "Okay folks, I'm going to read this last verse, and that is your question for the week. If you were God, would you punish?" Then after church some will say, "I thought God was just gracious."

**CRB:** "I don't come here to feel guilty. I feel guilty all week. I don't need to hear this here."

**WB:** I preached that text from Jeremiah at a church in Mississippi fairly recently, and after the service a guy came up to me and said, "That's a good text, but you added to it." I said, "Do you know what they call that? Adding to the text? They call that preaching." It's obviously very hard, especially for those who preach to the same congregation every week. But people have some sense that the prophetic question, "Shall I not punish them?" cannot carry any weight in a world organized without God as an active agent. Otherwise, what's the matter with catching poor people like birds in a cage? Can you think of any place where we have been catching poor people in cages? Or, more recently, catching undocumented children and putting them in cages?! I know it's easier to talk about it than it is to do it.

The study of prophetic texts is not simply a historical exercise. The texts have amazing contemporaneity when we have a little imagination about that. Much of Martin Luther King Jr.'s rhetoric of hope was basically rereading that middle part of the biblical book of Isaiah, which scholars call "Second Isaiah," which is set during the Babylonian exile and focuses less on judgment than on hope for those in exile. King depended very much on Second Isaiah for the new thing that God is going to do. In Second Isaiah, you can imagine God saying, "I have a dream."

# GRIEF AND THE TOTALISM

*Confessing Pain and Anger*

**CRB:** You say that the prophets are first and foremost art-
ists, which certainly rings true for King. They are poets
who, through their imaginative speech acts, articulate an
alternative world—alternative, that is, to the ideology of
the empire, which wants us to believe that it is the only
possible reality.

You sometimes describe the ideology or constructed
world of the empire as a "totalism." As I understand it, a
totalism is a constructed world that is totalitarian, that is,
it claims to totally comprehend and control everything
and everyone within it, to be the only possible world, to
be reality itself.

**WB:** That's right. I've beaten that term to death lately!

**CRB:** It's a helpful way to think about it, and our task as
pastors is, as you say, to expose the totalism, in all its
inadequateness, and to articulate an alternative to it. To
work creatively in community to find ways to crack it
open.

To borrow language from your now classic *Prophetic
Imagination* and your more recent *Reality, Grief, Hope,*
our task is to find ways, in our worship and preaching and teaching, to expose totalism as an ideology, to
grieve its brokenness, and to offer the gospel as an alternative reality over against it. The task is to expose reality

against the totalism of imperial ideology, give voice to grief against imperial denial when that ideology fails, and find hope against imperial despair in the wake of that failure.

I'm struck by the centrality of *grief* in this schema. This is a strong theme in your work on psalms of lament, which give voice to grief, pain, and disorientation. I once heard you say that perhaps we should get away from the confession of sin in worship and think of it more as an expression of lament, a time and space to grieve loss. Where does grief belong in the community? Where and how do we find ways to give voice to grief?

**WB:** Well, as you know, my long-term project has been to call for much more use of the lament psalms. I think the lament psalms need to be used regularly, and they need to be exposited so that people have some sense about what it is that we have to grieve. You know, most white congregations have to grieve that white privilege is over. Very many men have to grieve that male privilege is over. We have to grieve that.

I suspect that it's a very un-Calvinist thought that we ought to modify the confession of sin to do confessions of pain and grief and anger, much of which is rooted in sin, though not all of it. Sometimes, we are sinned against, and we need to confess that too.

I persuaded my Episcopal rector in Cincinnati where I worship to use four lament psalms for the four Sundays of Advent instead of the psalms prescribed by the lectionary. He did it, and I said to him, "I didn't know you

---

There is nothing more emancipatory than being able to tell the truth in a safe place.

could do that." He said, "You can either ask the Bishop's permission, or you can hope the Bishop doesn't find out." He did the latter. But we need to make it a recurring staple of our life with God, that the negations of our life need to be put in God's hands.

During a recent Wednesday night Lenten service in my church, we read Psalm 69, which is a long lament, and then everybody was given a three-by-five card on which to write out their grief and anger. Then everybody was invited to bring up their card, put it on God's table, and leave it there. And people actually did it! You cannot do that without using a lament psalm. So I think we need to recover that part of our Scripture. How come we never use the lament psalms anymore? Because we were seduced into thinking that the church ought to be the happiest place in town. The church doesn't need to be the happiest place in town. The church needs to be the most honest place in town. Out of such honesty, happiness arises. There is nothing more emancipatory than being able to tell the truth in a safe place.

# THE GODNESS OF GOD
## *Theology of Sin*

**CRB:** Here's another loaded term of faith: sin. You define it.

**WB:** Sin is a theological word, but we've turned it into a moral word. And it's hopeless when it becomes a moral category for a list of bad things. On the contrary, I think it means a refusal to accept the Godness of God (of which all these other things may be manifestations). So it's false faith. Martin Luther said that your god is whatever your heart clings to and relies on. Sin is having our hearts cling to what is false and letting our lives rely on what is phony and impotent. It's Americanism or the church or money, or any manifestation that my heart does not utterly rely on clinging to the God of the gospel. Because it's too hard! It's too hard for any of us. Barth has this long exposition on sin based on a reading of the story in Exodus of the golden calf, which he says is really the original sin in the narrative of Israel. And that sin was that they could not tolerate a God who was not palpably available to them. So they manufactured one.

In the liturgy, the Assurance of Pardon following the Confession of Sin is this astonishing declaration that God is willing and able to let us come back and utterly trust again.

# LITURGY VERSUS EMPIRE
*Elements of Worship*

**CRB:** Clearly we are not just talking about preaching here. We are talking about articulating an alternate world, against the totalism, through our entire church liturgy. I've heard you say that liturgy is a form of art that is about radical identity formation for the people of God. Can you say more about how liturgy creates an alternate world for us on Sundays?

**WB:** Yes. Consider how each component of the liturgy is a radical countercultural act. Think about the opening hymn: we always start with a hymn of praise, or *doxology*. Doxology is an incredible act of getting our minds off ourselves. It is an affirmation that our lives are rooted in a reference point other than ourselves. That is a huge countercultural act.

Think about the confession of sin. A confession of sin is an acknowledgment that we live in a world where forgiveness is available. That's very countercultural, because the *totalism* does not believe that anybody can ever be forgiven anything—your records and your debts follow you in perpetuity.

Think of the benediction. The way I like to say it is that the benediction is the affirmation that, when you leave this place, the force is with you. But totalism doesn't believe that there is any such force for life that can infuse our bodies. And think of the reading of Scripture, after which we say, "Thanks be to God!" That is a countercultural declaration that none of the other scripts that want to recruit us are the word of God. And we can be astonished that this alternative word of life is available to us one more time. You can think through all the elements of the liturgy in this way, as countercultural affirmations of an alternate reality.

I think you could even say it about church announcements, if you pressed it a little bit. Just think of the things that are announced. We announce that we're doing things nobody else does. You announce the youth fellowship meeting, where we'll gather senior high kids to help them be together in a fellowship of grace. My teenaged granddaughter is one of the coolest kids that go to school. She is so cool. Then she goes to youth fellowship on Sunday night, where being cool does not matter. And she loves it. She loves it first of all because the pastor knows her name, but she also loves it because she can let her guard down and she doesn't have to be cool. So the announcement of youth fellowship is that the cool kids can meet Sunday night to take a Sabbath from coolness. What a fellowship. What a love divine. It's astonishing.

One mode of truth-telling and witness-bearing is through the singing that is a specialty of the church. In my book titled *A Glad Obedience: Why and What We Sing*, I have probed how it is that we can (and must!) sing the extremities of our lives that we cannot otherwise say. We must do so, it turns out, in the public congregation in the presence of God. We will usefully recover such singing in the church that tells both judgment and hope, loss and possibility, that is, both Good Friday and Easter Sunday.

# PARADE OF LOSSES

*Eucharistic Empowerment*

**CRB:** You speak especially about the centrality of Communion, the Eucharist, in this regard, as being one of the most peculiar countercultural things we can do.

**WB:** Just think about the Eucharist, the name for which is the Greek word for "thanks." Do you know anywhere else except in the church where there could be a sacrament named "Thanks"? There is no gratitude in the totalism. If I say "thank you" to somebody in commerce, they don't say "you're welcome." They say "no problem." And I think, "Well, I didn't think it was a problem, but thanks anyway." But "thanks" means that I live by unmerited gifts. I do not live by my competence or my achievements or my possessions. That is very countercultural.

I get chill bumps during the Eucharist in my church when I see the priest hand the wafer to somebody. When you see people coming forward to avail themselves of the elements, when you see people coming forward, it is a parade of losses. And the priest knows almost all of them. And the bread and wine are an antidote to loss, because Communion says, "You're welcome." It says, "You're not alone." It says, "The holy power of God is here with us in this place, and all things are new."

So the transformation, the trans-substantiation in the Eucharist, is not turning bread to body or wine to blood. The transformation is about transforming the communicant into a new creation, because good food does that for us. So I think that people ought to walk away from the Communion table feeling ten feet tall in the face of the totalism of technological military consumerism.

# THICKNESS OF RELATIONSHIP
## Public Prayer

**CRB:** Let's talk about prayer. You have published two popular collections of your own prayers, *Awed to Heaven, Rooted in Earth* (2002) and *Prayers for a Privileged People* (2008). And like many of your former seminary students, I remember well your opening prayers in your classes. We were never late because we didn't want to miss them. They were very poetic and often had a surprising and provocative turn in the middle or end. I remember one in particular that went something like, "We walk through the mine fields, wondering when you might show up," as in to deliver us from danger, or perhaps to explode in our faces.

You don't usually offer extemporaneous prayers in public, right? You craft your prayers in writing, including those opening prayers in class. So can you talk about your intentions with those prayers? What shaped them? How did you go about preparing them?

**WB:** The danger with written prayer is that it becomes exhibitionist, and the danger with extemporaneous prayer is that it becomes a string of predictable clichés. So you have to try to somehow work between those. I am capable of an extemporaneous prayer, but with my students, I wanted to model prayer that required more energy and discipline than that.

My aim in most of those prayers was to create an environment and an awareness so that students would see that we are not primarily about an academic task here, but instead we are engaged in our life's work. I wanted to frame our class work in that way, with those prayers.

I think that public prayer is about creating a space for guided, authorized imagination about what the world feels like if we are really in contact with the God we know in Jesus. So what I tried to do in those classroom prayers was to take a theme or an image that was about to come in the lecture, and simply to walk around it awhile. What I don't like in public prayers are grocery lists, and that's what we do in many churches. I just don't like it, and I think it must bore God.

**CRB:** It was always interesting to me that you never began those prayers with a salutation, like "Dear God," or "Loving Father," or "Gracious God, . . ." Instead you would dive straight in, addressing God in the second person, as "you."

**WB:** I don't know whether it was a conscious decision on my part not to use such common formal addresses. I think they are excessively polite, and I have come to think that prayer is too urgent to monkey around with niceties. The extreme notion I have of address in prayer is that it is court trial language. So if you begin, "Oh Lord, Ruler of the universe, King of our hearts, Sovereign of the blah, blah, blah, blah," I think God says, "Have you got anything you want to ask me?" That may not be right, but I want to plunge in. I spent a lot of time on sabbatical in Cambridge, England, and my characterization of Anglican prayer is the prayer, "Oh Lord, deliver us from pomposity." I want to guard against that.

**CB:** What advice can you offer to church leaders about public prayer in church and other contexts? What is your theology of prayer?

**WB:** The theologian Karl Barth has written and said many things about prayer, but there are two that I love. One is that when he was asked why we pray, he said that we pray because we are commanded to pray. And the second is this amazing little sentence in the third volume of his *Church Dogmatics* in which he says that praying "is simply asking." Prayer is asking while recognizing that not one of us has adequate resources ourselves to get through the day.

We do bidding prayers in my church. We ask, we just keep asking. I understand what Barth means about prayer as asking, and I believe that. But any long relationship has to be more than asking. A long relationship has to be thick and rich and open. So I think that public prayer is acting out, as best we can, the thickness of that relationship.

So the center of prayer—and you can see it in the lament psalms—is petition. And our petitions sound so much like grocery lists. So I thought that in order for God not to respond to my petitions by saying, "Oh, I've heard all that before," I wanted to try to say it in a way that might be interesting to God. Because I think God loves words, as in the beginning was the word. So that's what I think.

I think that public prayer is about creating a space for guided, authorized imagination about what the world feels like if we are really in contact with the God we know in Jesus.

**CRB:** Some of your most influential work has been on the psalms, which for the church are public prayers of various kinds. You seem to keep returning to them.

**WB:** Yes, I do, I do. At the Festival of Homiletics in 2018, the general theme was "justice," to which nobody pays any attention in the Psalms. What I preached on was Psalm 10, and I talked about justice as a class war. The psalmist is describing how the wicked prosper at the expense of the poor, saying "there is no God" so we can do what we want. But then the poor summon God into the combat against them. So that's a psalm I've been walking around a lot lately. And, you know, there are many, many psalms I haven't done yet.

**CRB:** Do you have a favorite?

**WB:** Well my favorite psalm is 73.

**CRB:** Mine too! In my early twenties I was a campus ministry intern at University Presbyterian Church, which is on the campus of the University of Washington in Seattle. Our supervisor asked us interns to do a series of talks on the psalms, and I chose Psalm 73. I don't know why I picked that one exactly. But I feel like it was the first time that I really understood how in the psalms there is often a sudden turn, a change in the voice of the psalmist. In that one, the psalmist is lamenting how the wicked prosper and there seems to be no justice in the world. And then, out of nowhere, there is that pivot at verse 17: "until I went into the sanctuary of God" . . . And from there forward, the psalmist's whole perspective is completely transformed.

**WB:** It's so clear and decisive. Another favorite is Psalm 44, which we never use in church. It starts out with eight verses of praise and doxology, and then it launches into eight verses of assaults on God. You have sold us cheap!

You have made us a mockery! You have, you have, you have (vv. 9–14). Then verse 17 says, "Yet we have not forgotten you, or been false to your covenant." And then it ends with petitions. It's astounding. Israel can vigorously assault God; but then it turns, addressing God in hope-filled trust. But if we never use these psalms in the church, how will people know that's there?

# LEANING INTO A PRESENCE THAT VALORIZES
*Private Prayer*

**CRB:** We've talked about public prayer. What about personal or devotional prayer? Do you have a personal prayer life?

**WB:** I find my own personal prayer to be much more asking. I kind of keep a list of people for whom I have promised to pray, and I'm not very good at it, not very disciplined about it. I also know that my personal prayer is only partly verbal. The other part of my personal prayer is thanks. I am overwhelmed most often when I ponder the stream of inexplicable gifts in my life. Beyond such verbalizations, it is simply leaning into a presence that valorizes me. That amounts to something like the great hymn ending, "lost in wonder, love, and praise."

I come out of an economic and theological tradition in which it is not very easy to be valorized. I have to keep publishing and lecturing to try to valorize myself. So if I can step out of that narrative of not being valorized into the narrative of the grace of God, what I really want to do is just sit there. I don't have to say anything. I don't have to do anything. Just sit there. I'm not very good at it, because I keep being drawn back into that other narrative of needing to valorize myself.

As I mentioned earlier, I did a long stint of psychotherapy, many years, which wasn't very easy for me. But

I had this amazing therapist. And for fifty minutes he would just look at me and listen. He would just look. Once in a while, he would turn away and look at the clock, like he had to earn his $120 for the full hour or whatever. I never said anything, but if he looked away for three seconds, I was like, "Hey, over here!" So sitting in the presence feels as if God is looking and valorizing. God is not looking sternly, because when I would tell my therapist, "I haven't been able," he would always say, "You haven't been able yet." So God is looking hopefully, because, as it says in 1 John 3, it does not yet appear what we shall be like. But we know that we will be like Jesus. That's at best.

# MYSTERY OF AN
# ALTERNATE EXISTENCE
## *Sabbath Resistance to Brick Quotas*

**CRB:** What are your spiritual disciplines? What do you do to form, to shape your own spirituality?

**WB:** I'm not very good at spiritual discipline. It's all pretty conventional, and I really have to stay at it. Most days I spend a lot of time with the text. Part of that is my work. But I am so fortunate for my work to be so closely connected to my faith. And what I find when I write, which I do most days, is that I am very often surprised by what comes to me. My best way of meditating on a text is writing; for me, writing is a spiritual discipline.

Another form of spiritual discipline that I do not do as fully as I intend is justice work. I am connected to a couple of really serious justice enterprises in Cincinnati. I am committed to them and engaged with them, and that's part of my spiritual discipline.

I arrived at another part of my spiritual discipline when my younger son, John, who is probably the best theologian in the family, was about eight years old. One day he said to me, "For the way you talk, you sure do handle your money funny." It was sort of a wake-up call that my practices with money were not consistent with my talk about it. So the discipline of generosity is a part of my spiritual discipline and growth.

**CRB:** What about the spiritual discipline of Sabbath?

**WB:** Well, I talk a better game than I play.

**CRB:** You have written a wonderful little book on the subject called *Sabbath as Resistance: Saying No to the Culture of Now* (2014).

**WB:** I have, and I have come to the conclusion that the Sabbath is the most important of the commandments for us and the most difficult, and the reason it's so difficult is that we are caught in the totalism, and in the totalism there is no Sabbath. You have to be producing and consuming. And I'm very compromised about it, but I do work pretty intentionally at it. One of the decisions I have made is to blot out the NFL, and spectator sports generally. I use no energy or attentiveness on that, because I have come to the conclusion that it is an alternative liturgy, and I have no business participating in that alternative liturgy. I do participate in other alternative liturgies, so I'm not naive about that, but what I discovered is that by not participating in the NFL, I just have acres of time for a better Sabbath. I'm a work in progress about Sabbath.

**CRB:** Can you talk more about what you mean by "Sabbath as resistance"?

**WB:** I think that practicing Sabbath is a public, visible decision that my life is not defined by the rat race of production and consumption. And I think that our children and our grandchildren need to see us engaging in that act of resistance because we are a different kind of people. In Isaiah 56, when the people return to Jerusalem from exile in Babylon, they had a big argument about who were the real Jews. Who is "us" and who is "other"? What about eunuchs and foreigners, for example? Should they be included? Isaiah 56 is an argument that they should be, that they should worship with "us."

And what astonishes me about that text is that the only specific requirement to qualify for worship is that you have to keep Sabbath. There's a generic requirement to practice covenant, but the only specific one is that you have to get out of the rat race enough to be present to the mystery of an alternate existence. That gives me chills.

The totalism of market ideology wants always to crowd in on Sabbath and make us consumers and producers. The astonishing affirmation of Sabbath is that the reason they left Egypt is that they didn't want their life to be defined by meeting brick quotas. I live a life of brick quotas—how many articles have I written lately? And I do think that if I can just spend a couple hours doing that on Sunday afternoon, I'll get another journal article finished. Those are my bricks. But then I am caught up short by the recognition that the world is not waiting for another brick from me. Still, it's hard. It's hard because we get our self-esteem and self-respect and so on from getting one more thing done.

I think it is crucial for baptized Christians to recognize that our baptism, which is our act of peculiar identity, is in deep tension with the pressure of the totalism that wants to identify us otherwise. Jewish tradition has always understood that the maintenance of Jewish identity requires huge intentionality. We now live in a culture in which maintaining a serious Christian identity requires huge intentionality as well. That wasn't true when I was growing up; everybody was more or less on board. But it is true now. Sabbath is one of those acts of intentionality whereby we remind ourselves of who we really are.

I think that practicing Sabbath is a public, visible decision that my life is not defined by the rat race of production and consumption. And I think that our children and our grandchildren need to see us engaging in that act of resistance because we are a different kind of people.

**CRB:** We talk pretty easily about nine of the commandments. But we giggle when we talk about the fourth commandment, to "remember the sabbath day, and keep it holy" (Exod. 20:8). The possibility of actually taking rest, refusing to do anything productive, seems impossible, even absurd. As a church, we really have no idea.

**WB:** That's right. In an article called "Quitting the Paint Factory," Mark Slouka recalls dinner parties in Manhattan where very often the conversation turns to people bragging about how little sleep they get so that they can get more work done. He describes them as worshiping at "the Church of Work." He went on in the article to say that if you stay tired all the time, if you are members of the Church of Work, then you do not have any energy for critical reflection. And when you have a society without critical reflection, he said, you are on the way to fascism. I agree that we are on the way to fascism in our society, and Sabbath is an act of resistance against that.

# COUNTERING TECHNOLOGICAL MILITARY CONSUMERISM

## *Neighborliness*

**CRB:** So there are numerous books published by the Alban Institute and other publishers like them about vital congregations and healthy leadership. What do you say are the marks of a healthy congregation?

**WB:** I have no expertise about that. I would say good preaching, good music, good food, good ministry. And when you talk, for example, about the emergent church movement, I think the emergent church is simply a discovery that much of the baggage that churches carry is really kind of irrelevant. And we just use too much energy on that. You can very soon get into an argument between a liberal and a conservative about whether justice work needs to be done through the government or through the private sector. And the answer to that is, "Yes! Always. Everywhere. Yes." It's really not either-or. I think that we really have to work in the church to see that liberal Christians and conservative Christians are on the same side of the issue against what I call technological consumer militarism. The threat is not that conservative Christianity is a threat to liberals or vice versa. The threat is technological military consumerism. We have been entrusted with an alternative to that, around which liberals and conservatives ought to be able to rally together.

**CRB:** Can you unpack that threat—"technological military consumerism"?

**WB:** Well, we all know about consumerism, right? I think the reason that we have such a defense budget in this country, a shameless defense budget, is that we have to maintain our leverage in the world to maintain our high standard of consumerism. That is, we have got to control the forces and markets that properly belong to other people. We have to control them, or our standard of living is going to go down. So that's our militarism, which saturates everything in our common life and is obviously tied to our consumerism. Then there is the technological part, by which I mean the belief that there are quick fixes to everything if we're just smart enough and fast enough and rich enough. And within that mindset, we don't have to take the trouble of long-term engagement with each other. That's what I mean by technological. We can see this in so much television advertising, especially concerning medical technology: "Get the next drug that is new and improved!"

I will not quibble about those particular terms. But that social reality, however one names it, leads to a shriveling of the human spirit. And we're going to die from it; we're going to die as a society if that is fully the order of the day. The reduction of life to consumerism and technology, protected by an inordinate militarism, will kill us. The signs of that dying are everywhere around us. The church is called to keep reminding people that there is another way to organize our social relationships.

---

The reduction of life to consumerism and technology, protected by an inordinate militarism, will kill us.

---

That way is harder and slower and more demanding, but it is the truth of our life.

**CRB:** In *Journey to the Common Good* (2010), one of the issues of non-neighborliness is our exhaustion. We're too tired to care for our neighbor. So then we become even more isolated, and we can only care for ourselves. Exhaustion prevents neighborliness. So, related to what you were saying about Sabbath, neighborliness requires restedness.

Our church wants to be and has been a good neighbor in our community of Park Hill in Denver. We talk a lot and do a lot of work around how we can be better neighbors. Last summer we read your *Journey to the Common Good* and it led to some good conversations. One of the themes that grabbed us was how fear and anxiety are antithetical to neighborliness. That resonates with many of us. Can you say more? What is your wisdom for communities of faith as we strive to get outside of our own fear and anxiety?

**WB:** You know what that means locally better than I do. But I think it generally means to be in face-to-face contact with people who are unlike us, and that's not very easy for anyone.

I also have decided of late that neighborliness means to be signed on with community organizing efforts that are present in every city, because part of the anti-neighborliness is simply that we don't know each other, and part of the anti-neighborliness are structures and policies that keep us from engaging with one another. So some muscle must be organized at the level of policy and strategy. I myself am sort of connected with a community organizing where I live, and their strategy is "fifty-two and one": you go to church fifty-two Sundays a year, and once a year you ask everybody to show up at city hall for one issue, which they call an action. You'd be surprised how hard it is to get folks to do that, but their experience is that if you can mobilize a mass of people, the authorities will pay attention. In Lexington, Kentucky, they had an action and they went to city hall to ask for $200,000 for low-income housing. They didn't get it. So they mobilized 4,000 people and went back to city hall once again. The leader had been trained to expect that, when he asked the mayor, the mayor would say no, and then he should keep asking. But when he asked the mayor the second time, the mayor said yes. And then he went right on with his training and asked the mayor again and again. He didn't hear the yes! He was so surprised at the yes.

I think that bodily political engagement is really important for democratic functioning. It isn't even civil disobedience; it's just showing up. And I think it is a function of neighborliness to show up and say, "Here I am. I personally don't need city hall to change anything. I'm doing fine. But I'm here on behalf of my neighbors for whom things are not fine."

I don't think it's an either-or between face-to-face engagement with those not like us and public action. It's always a both-and. But it's very hard, because most of us church people have been schooled otherwise. So the way I frame that for myself is that I don't mind dying for Christ—I'm ready to do that—but I don't want to be inconvenienced, and neighborliness is just inconvenient.

# ECONOMIES OF EXTRACTION
*Money and Possessions from Exodus to Today*

**CRB:** I really would like to hear you talk about that book that's sitting on my desk: *Money and Possessions*, recently published in the Interpretation Resources series from Westminster John Knox.

**WB:** What I did was to offer an introductory chapter about the incessant materiality of faith in the Bible, from creation to incarnation. The Bible begins with God's generative love for the world, the real plant-producing, life-sustaining earth. And then Jesus came in the flesh to love the world. The real world cared for by God and the flesh of Jesus attest that God cares about material reality, with all of its economic palpability. But the church too often has preferred things "spiritual" and "otherworldly," as though the material world were dispensable. The Bible is an insistence that the material world is God's big preoccupation. The inescapable outcome of that claim is that the bodily well-being of the neighbor is a primary task of our life in God's world.

Then, following my introduction, I laid down six theses that are fairly obvious, and then I just started working my way through the biblical text, from Genesis through to Revelation, with that focus on materiality. Obviously I had to be very selective.

**CRB:** It is a thick book!

**WB:** Yes. I was just doing exposition through the text, but when I finished the book, I became aware that an argument had emerged with two core theses. The first thesis is that the Bible characteristically emerged in economies of extraction, whereby wealth was being extracted from the vulnerable by the powerful, by means of regressive taxation, low wages, high interest rates, rigged loan arrangements, and wholesale privatization (which is a "free pass" for the privileged). And the second thesis is, obviously, that the Bible proposes an alternative economy to the economy of extraction. That's in a nutshell what I argued. It runs from the Exodus narrative, Deuteronomy, and the prophets through Jesus and Paul and James and Revelation. The litmus test for a viable economy is always "widow, orphan, immigrant"! It covers the whole Bible. The main dissenting voice, I think, is probably the book of Proverbs, which has at least some texts that are much more about a settled economy than that. But I was really astonished about the cumulative force of it.

---

The litmus test for a viable economy is always "widow, orphan, immigrant"! It covers the whole Bible.

---

**CRB:** Do any specific examples come to mind?

**WB:** Having read Ellen F. Davis's *Biblical Prophecy* (2014), published in the same series, I was struck by Ezekiel 27–28, in which the prophet takes the coastal city of Tyre, a commercial powerhouse, as a paradigmatic example of market commoditization. In that economy everything and everyone is reduced to a commodity that

can be bought, sold, or traded. The text names all the
products for which Tyre traded, and it's a list of Hebrew
words that I don't know. What's interesting is, in 27:13,
as it goes along listing products, it includes "human
beings." And then in Revelation 18—this is what I
got from Ellen Davis—we find critique of the great
city of Babylon has an abbreviated version of the same
list from Ezekiel. And there again, in verse 13, listed
along with various other products is "human beings."
That is, human beings, reduced to slavery, are in the
inventory of marketable goods as just another tradable
commodity. Likewise in our economy, the lives of the
vulnerable (poor people, people of color, immigrants)
are also very "cheap." The lives of the vulnerable, in our
commodity-propelled economy, do not merit attention,
support, or viability. That social reality is reflected, as
it no doubt was in ancient Tyre, in both practice and
policy.

So the commodification of human persons in biblical
narrative begins with slavery in Egypt under Pharaoh,
and continues under King Solomon, and then into the
Babylonian exile, and then into the postexilic period, as
we can see in Nehemiah 9, in one of Ezra's great prayers
(it's a long prayer). At the end he says, "Here we are,
slaves to this day—slaves in the land that you gave to our
ancestors to enjoy its fruit and its good gifts. Its rich yield
goes to the kings whom you have set over us because
of our sins; they have power also over our bodies and
over our livestock at their pleasure" (Neh. 9:36–37a).
And this is the way it ends: "and we are in great dis-
tress" (v. 37b). They were being taxed by the Persians,
who had conquered the Babylonians and helped them
begin rebuilding Jerusalem. So the commodification of

human beings runs through the whole Old Testament narrative.

This practice of extraction running through the Bible is such an obvious, easy transfer to our economy of extraction, for which the healthcare debate is a perfect embodiment. But by and large, I do not think pastors know those texts, because they're not in the lectionary. The lectionary committees leave them out. And if you don't know the texts then you cannot make the connections.

**WB:** So the text that I have been working a lot on lately, just for fun, is the story of Zacchaeus the tax collector in Luke 19. Zacchaeus says, "If I have defrauded," and he certainly did, "then I will repay them fourfold." And Jesus says something like, "Salvation has come to your house this day." And then he says, "You are a son of Abraham." And I think the story is set up for Zacchaeus to say, "Ahh! I forgot! I forgot I'm a Jew! I thought I was a tax collector for Rome!" So the preachable point is that Christians in the commodity economy have forgotten their baptism, and the recovery of our baptism is so urgent. Because if the church were to recover baptism, the dominant culture could not withstand that. But we are so feeble in our resolve.

**CRB:** You have always been interested in socioeconomic critique—Marxist social theory and ideological criticism, for example. But your work on money and possessions in the Bible seems to have taken you in a somewhat different direction, paying more attention to economic theory and the history of capitalism.

**WB:** That's right. Which is a direction I might not have pursued without taking up that project. What I think is worth asking is, How did the church develop the habit of missing all of that? I think it's not only that church members don't know it's there. I don't think most pastors know it's there either. And, again, the lectionary very carefully screens all these passages out.

**CRB:** When you spoke at my former church, I remember you handing out a one-page annotated bibliography of five books on capitalism and economic theory that you think all church people should be reading. I recall it included Sven Beckert's *Empire of Cotton* (2014), which traces the history of capitalism by following the cotton industry, and Thomas Piketty's *Capital in the Twenty-first Century* (2014), which uses massive amounts of data to show the rise of inequality under capitalism. I remember thinking, first of all, wow, you have a voracious hunger for learning, and, second of all, wow, the church needs to get serious about studying economics.

**WB:** Yes it does! Another of the five books was Saskia Sassen's *Expulsions: Brutality and Complexity in the Global Economy* (2014). It is loaded with statistics about how the powerful are extracting land, chemical resources, and water from poor people. Sassen includes a very famous quote from the president of Nestle about selling bottled water. He says, "You have to price water or people will not recognize how valuable it is." Astonishing. In our society "expulsion" often takes the form of mass incarceration. Or to cite a most recent case, the US government has just opposed an action of the world community that would champion breast feeding of infants. The US position is to protect American firms that sell baby formula, even though it has long been proven that baby formula is less healthy than breast feeding. The championing of baby formula is not far removed from Nestle selling bottled water! In that most recent governmental action, not only is the commodity of baby formula championed, but the babies are turned into market commodities. All of that fits broadly under Sassen's rubric of "expulsion."

Now what I puzzle about is how in the world you ever get church people to be able to see this whole picture, because all you do on Sundays is just offer bits and pieces. That's all you get to do.

**CRB:** One hour a week maybe.

**WB:** And there's not enough retention from one week to the next to be connecting dots, which of course is what makes teaching in adult education and in midweek studies so important. It really requires sustained teaching. But most solo pastors don't have any energy left for teaching, because you just get gobbled up by all the other demands.

**CRB:** And in small churches, if you have even a few vocal opponents, it really can stifle this kind of important work.

**WB:** We think we cannot afford to lose them.

**CRB:** True, and that can quickly dilute the whole conversation.

# WHAT IS OLD AND WHAT IS NEW
## *When Do We Cease to Be Church?*

**CRB:** I'm just going to ask you to define a number of words that we use in Christianity, that we use in the church, that I think people trip over when reclaiming faith language that we're not comfortable with. So what does the church mean to you? We were talking about this at our membership committee the other night, and people were saying, what does it mean, and why join?

**WB:** Well I'm not a single-minded person about the church, but I'll make two responses. One is that Luther said, "Wherever the Word is rightly preached and the sacraments rightly celebrated," that's the church. To which I think Moltmann said you have to add wherever diaconate service is being done. So that's one side of my thought.

But I am also deeply committed to the on-going institutional structure of the church, because I believe it is the carrier of the catholic tradition, and the catholic tradition protects us from sectarian goofiness—all these people that want to start new churches that are not connected to anything. I think the danger of sectarianism is very great, and I think there's great importance in sustaining institutional structures. I also agree with the Calvinist phrase about the church being "reformed and always reforming." The structures of the church always need to be reformed in radical ways, but I do not want to minimize the historic connectivity of the institutional church.

**CRB:** When do we cease being church? Is it when we stop preaching the Word, celebrating the sacraments, and caring for those in need?

**WB:** I don't know that I would defend this, but I think we stop being a church when we give up what the doctrine of the Trinity means to confess. I didn't say, when we give up the doctrine of the Trinity, but what the doctrine of the Trinity means to confess about the inter-linkage of Jesus as "God from God, light from light, true God from true God, begotten not made, of one being with the Father." I think that's nonnegotiable. I have a hard time with that. I would rather talk about the humanity of Jesus, but I think if we give that up we become an ethical society in which there is no gospel, no good news. Of course, once you go down that path with one pastor, then the next pastor after that one is even worse and worse and worse and worse. It's probably beyond recovery, given who joins the church for those reasons. So I think the stuff that is intended to be claimed in the creeds is terribly important, and of course that relates to the continuity of the institutional structure: the structure of the church keeps the creeds, and if it didn't, I think we would all be lost. So because of this insistence that we confess, the story of God is peculiarly writ via the story of Jesus. And I don't think that's very easy.

I also think our reasoning, our confessional reasoning, is not from the Father to the Son. It's from the Son to the Father. So if you see Jesus, then you know who the Father is. It's not that you start knowing the Father and then you say, "Oh, that's the Son." It's the other way around, I think.

**CRB:** It is sometimes argued that those creeds about the Trinity and Jesus, which come from a time when Christianity really had become synonymous with the Roman Empire, are examples of that Greek static universalism we were just talking about. I agree that can't really be the church without confessing this doctrine, but how do we do so without falling back into the seduction of static universalism?

**WB:** We have to remember that our best confessional statements are inescapably poetic. When we reduce that poetry and imagine it as a prose proposition, it then comes out as universal truth that contains all and becomes totalizing. That, of course, is not what the church intended its formulations of the creeds to be. They functioned as a confession to withstand the claims of empire. When the poetry is reduced, it takes on the dialect of empire and no longer serves as risky confession.

**CRB:** Do you know Richard Rohr?

**WB:** Oh yes, I correspond with him and was with him recently. He does such important work and is a lodestar for me, as he is for many others.

**CRB:** His recent work has focused on the doctrine of the Trinity, reframing but also reclaiming Trinity and the Godhead and the dynamic relationship of the three persons in some creative ways that pick up on earlier Catholic thinkers like Teilhard de Chardin.

**WB:** Well, I do think it has to be very imaginatively interpreted, as the church has always done, so that's what I think. The supportive biblical text is at the end of

Matthew 13, when Jesus says that the scribe training for the kingdom of heaven is like a householder who takes from his treasure both what is old and what is new. I think that is just the endless dynamic of the historical process. I think we have certain times when we are mandated to be venturesome. And then we arrive at a moment when some reformer says that we've gone too far now, and we have to come back to basics. That is an inevitable dynamic process.

**CRB:** I agree.

**WB:** But all that is beyond my pay grade.

**CRB:** So why join a church? What is the benefit of church membership? That's another conversation that a lot of mainline Protestant ministers and leaders are having. Other than voting to elect officers or to be an officer, or being on a search committee for the next pastor, or things like that, why is membership important?

**WB:** It is about being a member of a body that has things in common, and that has futures in common toward which we are willing to work. Each member is invited to take sustained responsibility for the life and well-being of the whole. That responsibility must be widely held. It is not primarily a matter of the institution, but of the community for which the institution is an indispensable placeholder. The time is well over in our society when it could be assumed that the church is simply "there" and can be counted on at our convenience. Now we know how fragile the church as a community is, and that it therefore requires attentiveness on the part of all of its members. I imagine people will say, "Well, I can do that without signing on." But I think membership gives expression to obligation. It obligates us to each other. This is very soft in the congregation where I am. Someone says to a pastor, "I'd like to be a member of the congregation," and the pastor says, "Well, if you want to be, you are." I think that's weak. There needs to be, in my judgment, acclamation of membership and the taking of mutual vows as a process for signing on for mutual obligation. It is not a matter of law or rule, but of world-making ritual performance.

**CRB:** Do we need to raise the bar?

**WB:** I don't think the bar for membership has to be high. But I think it has to be intentional. I don't care if it's a low bar, but I want to know, "Do you want to be a part of this? Then say yes." It's the same argument about why get married? Why not just have a partnership? Because marriage is participating in a kind of public forum that is sustaining and to which one is accountable.

# BELIEVING IN

## *The Relationality of Faith*

**CRB:** You tend to use the language of "confession" rather than "belief." It seems like this word has become a stumbling block for many people, who see it as being a kind of truth claim or point of argument over against other beliefs.

**WB:** I think behind belief is trust. Trust is obviously a relational category, and my understanding is that the language of belief is trying to give a cognitive articulation to that in which we trust. Unfortunately, what has happened in the church is that belief has become a substitute for trust rather than an expression of it. And then we argue about beliefs as propositions, competing truth claims, which is a waste of time. But when we say "the one in whom we believe," I think then we are really saying "the one in whom we trust." And it's too bad that the trust dimension got siphoned off into propositional language, because that trust dimension of belief is indispensable. The language of "confession" means to stand up in public and make declaration about one's intention, which entails obligation and cost. Or, as we say in the UCC, it concerns "cost and joy."

**CRB:** The Latin behind the "I believe in," which starts our creeds, is *credo in*, which can be translated something like "I set my heart in." That is profoundly relational language. That's trust language. Now, what about "faith" language? How does it relate?

**WB:** Well then "faith" is a two-pronged word that can mean trust or belief. It seems to me it contains all of that. So having faith is naming the one in whom I trust. Luther has a marvelous way to put it: that which your heart clings to and relies upon, that is your God. But obviously the faith of the church has been packaged in doctrinal formulation. So in Baptism, the Episcopal liturgy asks the candidate or the parents of the candidate, "do you believe in God the father," and then you recite the first article of the creed. Then the next question, "do you believe in the Son," and then you recite the second article, and so on. So belief is an attempt to attest the one in whom we have faith. But it comes out propositionally. I think we do a very poor job of helping people see that complexity.

---

Belief is an attempt to attest the one in whom we have faith. But it comes out propositionally. I think we do a very poor job of helping people see that complexity.

---

**CRB:** Absolutely. We also stand as a congregation and recite the Nicene Creed when we do baptisms. And I look out there and see so many people not reciting it. It looks intentional, like they're refusing to, because they would feel hypocritical or inauthentic if they were to say the words, or at least some of the words. And part of that has to be because they see this language as propositional truth language rather than as relational trust language.

**WB:** We have to guide them into reading it back into poetry. I heard about an Episcopal priest who, once a year or every other year, when they confess the creed, he asks people to stand up whenever they are saying something they believe and to sit down whenever they are saying something they don't believe. Of course that is a foolish exercise, because a confessional statement is not subject to vote. I would wager that people "choosing" what they do or do not believe is to see how faith claims can be made to conform to Enlightenment rationality—surely a hopeless assignment. Better to use our time on education so that people can enter into the rich claims of the poetic language. One does not, after all, vote on poetry. Rather one listens to it attentively, over and over.

# JUSTICE AND REFORMATION
## *What Keeps You Going*

**CRB:** What keeps you going? You still study and write every day. You're still putting things out there that are shaping the conversation. What is it that drives you?

**WB:** Partly I don't have anything else to do.

**CRB:** I know you say that. That's tongue in cheek, though.

**WB:** Not entirely. Unfortunately, I think it is this relentless work ethic. I have to be useful.

It also helps to be a bit compulsive. I think it is honest to say that I am compelled by my sense of vocation as a scholar and interpreter. But quite specifically, I find work in the biblical text to be endlessly energizing. While I continue to work the same themes over again, I always find fresh aspects and new rich linkages to our own life and faith. Of course it helps a great deal to have what I sense to be a receptive, if modest, "public" in the life of the church that in various ways receives and makes some use of my work.

It's the most satisfying thing I do, hard as it is. But I'm getting close to the end of my energy, so we'll see.

**CRB:** What scholarly contributions do you think you'll be remembered for? What do you expect will have the most influence?

**WB:** The late Gerhard von Rad once said that he hoped he would be remembered as a good reader of texts. That's pretty good. I think my durable scholarly contribution is the schema of orientation/disorientation/new orientation, which I worked out especially in the psalms. I think that will last because it works on so many fronts.

**CRB:** I keep fighting for that "structure legitimatization" and "embrace of pain" framework that you worked out in those two articles in the *Catholic Biblical Quarterly*. I still think that is just so useful.

**WB:** Yes. That's a really important articulation for me. I don't know that those articles have been much noticed, but they're there. So who knows? I don't know. I suppose my work will have to speak for itself and see what endures, if anything, because it really is quite remarkable how, I suppose in many fields but in our field especially, how quickly work is forgotten. I mean, who in the younger scholars even knows who Albright was? We thought he was a king for a little while.

**CRB:** So, Walter, relatedly, what are *you* most proud of in your career?

**WB:** Oh, my students. Tim (Beal) and Tod (Linafelt) and Davis (Hankins) particularly, and some others. Also some very good pastors. And beyond that, you know, a couple of my books, certainly *The Prophetic Imagination*. I think my early articulation of "abundance and scarcity" will persist because it focuses the Bible on material concerns. I think my notion of "core testimony" and "countertestimony" is durable, even if it takes forms well beyond my own imagination. The idea was to stress the trajectories of biblical faith that continue in deep tension with each other in a way that refuses the reductionism of the Bible to a safe package—a temptation of some forms of "canonical" interpretation. And I think my early championing of imagination is a significant marker for our discipline as it moves beyond the imagined objectivity of historical criticism to the recognition of the generative work of specific interpretive communities. I am proud of the fact that I did my critical work for the sake of the church, specifically for the equipping of pastors.

I am proud of the fact that I did my critical work for the sake of the church, specifically for the equipping of pastors.

**CRB:** You mentioned the other day that you wrote a draft of your obituary. I don't think many people work on their own obituary. Then again, you're talking with someone who's been planning her funeral since she was in her late teens. When I read a text or hear a hymn I like, I'll think, "I want that one in my funeral! Don't forget that one!" As a pastor I tell people that when they hear or read something they might like for their funeral, they should write it down so they don't forget. I mean, I like that you are working on your obituary. I think it's really healthy for all of us to do that, to work on our own services, to work on what you hope people will remember about you.

**WB:** Yes. It's a kind of reflection on what your life adds up to and all that. We had a funeral of an old man at our church two weeks ago and the pastor said he had written his funeral service out in 1993, and he picked eleven hymns. We didn't sing them all.

I have enough health problems that I am aware of my mortality. I don't think it's imminent, but if I hit a few more glass doors, as I did at the hotel in Denver when

I last visited you and Tim, it might be! So I wanted to work on it in a way that I could process it with my wife, Tia, and so on.

**CRB:** Say more about that. How did it go?

**WB:** I wrote a first draft of it. I said that I think my two theological tasks have been social justice and the reformation of the church—or urging that the church should come to terms with its real identity. Until I wrote that draft, I had not seen that those two accents have been definitional for me and my work. My other fresh awareness was that I stand in a long line of German Pietists mediated to me through my father. That tradition was fairly simple ("innocent") in its theology: "Love Jesus and care for the vulnerable neighbor." In the work of the draft of my obituary, I came to a good list of unresolved regrets, both personal and professional (that will not be reported on). But I also know and trust that God's grace abounds, even amid a host of regrets.

# WORKS CITED AND
# FURTHER READING

Anderson, John E. *Jacob and the Divine Trickster: A Theology of Deception and YHWH's Fidelity to the Ancestral Promise in the Jacob Cycle.* University Park, PA: Eisenbrauns, 2011.

Beckert, Sven. *Empire of Cotton: A Global History.* New York: Penguin Random House, 2014.

Boer, Roland. *The Sacred Economy of Ancient Israel.* Louisville, KY: Westminster John Knox Press, 2015.

Borg, Marcus J. *Reading the Bible Again for the First Time: Taking the Bible Seriously but Not Literally.* New York: HarperCollins, 2001.

Brueggemann, Walter. *Awed to Heaven, Rooted in Earth: Prayers of Walter Brueggemann.* Philadephia: Fortress, 2002.

———. *The Bible Makes Sense.* Reprint edition. Louisville, KY: Westminster John Knox Press, 2001.

———. *Finally Comes the Poet: Daring Speech for Proclamation.* Philadelphia: Fortress, 1989.

———. *A Glad Obedience: Why and What We Sing.* Louisville, KY: Westminster John Knox Press, 2019.

———. *Journey to the Common Good.* Louisville, KY: Westminster John Knox Press, 2010.

———. *The Land: Place as Gift, Promise, and Challenge in Biblical Faith.* Philadelphia: Fortress, 1977.

———. *The Message of the Psalms: A Theological Commentary.* Philadelphia: Fortress, 1984.

———. *Money and Possessions.* Louisville, KY: Westminster John Knox Press, 2016.

———. *Prayers for a Privileged People*. Nashville: Abingdon, 2008.

———. *The Prophetic Imagination*. Philadelphia: Fortress, 1978.

———. *Reality, Grief, Hope: Three Urgent Prophetic Tasks*. Grand Rapids: Eerdmans, 2014.

———. *Sabbath as Resistance: Saying No to the Culture of Now*. Louisville, KY: Westminster John Knox Press, 2014.

———. "A Shape for Old Testament Theology, I: Structure Legitimation." *Catholic Biblical Quarterly* 47 (1985): 28–46.

———. "A Shape for Old Testament Theology, II: Embrace of Pain." *Catholic Biblical Quarterly* 47 (1985): 395–415.

———. *Theology of the Old Testament: Testimony, Dispute, Advocacy*. Philadelphia: Fortress, 1997.

———, and Hans Walter Wolff. *The Vitality of Old Testament Traditions*. 2nd ed. Atlanta: John Knox Press, 1982.

Buber, Martin. *I and Thou*. Edinburgh: T & T. Clark, 1937.

Davis, Ellen F. *Biblical Prophecy: Perspectives for Christian Theology, Discipleship, and Ministry*. Louisville, KY: Westminster John Knox Press, 2014.

Gimbel, Steven. *Einstein's Jewish Science: Physics at the Intersection of Politics and Religion*. Baltimore: Johns Hopkins University Press, 2012.

Gottwald, Norma K. *The Tribes of Yahweh: A Sociology of the Religion of Liberated Israel 1250–1050 B.C.E.* Maryknoll: Orbis Press, 1979.

Gunkel, Hermann. *Schöpfung und Chaos in Urzeit und Endzeit: Eine religionsgeschichtliche Untersuchung über Gen 1 und Ap Joh 12*. Göttingen: Vandenhoeck and Ruprecht, 1895.

Horsley, Richard A. *Jesus and Empire: The Kingdom of God and the New World Disorder*. Minneapolis: Fortress Press, 2003.

———. *In the Shadow of Empire: Reclaiming the Bible as a History of Faithful Resistance*. Louisville, KY: Westminster John Knox Press, 2008.

Levinas, Emmanuel. *Totality and Infinity: An Essay on Exteriority*. Pittsburgh: Duquesne University Press, 1969.

Meeks, Douglas. *God the Economist: The Doctrine of God and Political Economy*. Minneapolis: Fortress Press, 1989.

Moltmann, Jürgen. *The Crucified God: The Cross of Christ as the Foundation and Criticism of Christian Theology*. Trans. R. A. Wilson. Minneapolis: Fortress, 1993.

——. *Theology of Hope: On the Ground and the Implications of a Christian Eschatology*. Trans. James W. Leitch. Minneapolis: Fortress, 1993.

Niebuhr, Reinhold. *Moral Man and Immoral Society: A Study in Ethics and Politics*. New York: Charles Scribner's Sons, 1932.

——. *The Nature and Destiny of Man: A Christian Interpretation*. New York: Charles Scribner's Sons, 1941.

Piketty, Thomas. *Capital in the Twenty-First Century*. Translated by Arthur Goldhammer. Cambridge, MA: Harvard University Press, 2014.

Reclaiming Jesus. A Confession of Faith in a Time of Crisis. http://reclaimingjesus.org.

Sassen, Saskia. *Expulsions: Brutality and Complexity in the Global Economy*. Cambridge, MA: Harvard University Press, 2014.

Scott, James C. *Domination and the Arts of Resistance: Hidden Transcripts*. New Haven, CT: Yale University Press, 1990.

——. *Weapons of the Weak: Everyday Forms of Peasant Resistance*. New Haven, CT: Yale University Press, 1985.

Slouka, Mark. "Quitting the Paint Factory: On the Virtues of Idleness." *Harper's Magazine* 309:1854 (November 2004): 57–65.

Wellhausen, Julius. *Prolegomena to the History of Israel*. Translated by A. Sutherland Black and Allen Menzies. Edinburgh: Allen and Charles Black, 1885.

Winnicott, Donald W. *The Child, the Family, and the Outside World*. New York: Penguin 1973.

CPSIA information can be obtained
at www.ICGtesting.com
Printed in the USA
LVHW030225021019
632824LV00011B/58